CW00369544

Secrets of Success:
Getting into Medical School

Secrets of Success: Getting into Medical School

Edited by

Viyaasan Mahalingasivam BMedSci
*Final year Medical Student, Barts and The London School of
Medicine and Dentistry, London, UK*

Marc A Gladman MBBS PhD MRCOG MRCS(Eng)
*UKCRC Clinical Lecturer in Surgery, Centre for Academic Surgery,
Institute of Cell and Molecular Science, Barts and The London School
of Medicine and Dentistry, London, UK*

Manoj Ramachandran BSc MBBS MRCS(Eng) FRCS(Tr&Orth)
*Consultant Trauma and Orthopaedic Surgeon, Barts and The
London NHS Trust, London, and Honorary Senior Lecturer, William
Harvey Research Institute, Barts and The London School of Medicine
and Dentistry, London, UK*

The ROYAL
SOCIETY *of*
MEDICINE
PRESS *Limited*

Published by the Royal Society of Medicine Press Ltd
1 Wimpole Street, London W1G 0AE, UK
Tel: +44 (0)20 7290 2921
Fax: +44 (0)20 7290 2929
E-mail: publishing@rsmpress.co.uk

British Library Cataloguing in Publication Data
A catalogue record for this book is available from the British Library

ISBN: 978-1-85315- 837-7

Distribution in Europe and Rest of the World:
Marston Book Services Ltd
PO Box 269
Abingdon
Oxon OX14 4YN, UK
Tel: +44 (0)1235 465500
Fax: +44 (0)1235 465555
Email: direct.order@marston.co.uk

Distribution in USA and Canada:
Royal Society of Medicine Press Ltd
c/o BookMasters Inc
30 Amberwood Parkway
Ashland, OH 44805, USA
Tel: +1 800 247 6553/ +1 800 266 5564
Fax: +1 410 281 6883
Email: order@bookmasters.com

Distribution in Australia and New Zealand:
Elsevier Australia
30–52 Smidmore Street
Marrickville NSW 2204, Australia
Tel: +61 2 9517 8999
Fax: +61 2 9517 2249
Email: service@elsevier.com.au

Typeset by IMH(Cartrif), eh20 9dx, Scotland, UK
Printed in the UK by Bell & Bain, Glasgow, UK

Contents

Contributors

Ahmed Aber BSc Final year medical student, Barts and The London School of Medicine and Dentistry, London, UK

Yousef Basma BSc Final year medical student, Barts and The London School of Medicine and Dentistry, London, UK

Omar Chehab BSc Final year medical student, Barts and The London School of Medicine and Dentistry, London, UK

Gosagan Gopalakrishnan BSc MRChB Basic Surgical Training Year 2, London Deanery, London, UK

Pairaw Kader BMedSci Final year medical student, Barts and The London School of Medicine and Dentistry, London, UK

Susannah Love BA BMBS Foundation Year 2, Southend University Hospital NHS Foundation Trust, Westcliff-on-Sea, UK

Samir Matloob BMedSci Final year medical student, Barts and The London School of Medicine and Dentistry, London, UK

Veena Naganathar BMedSci Final year medical student, Barts and The London School of Medicine and Dentistry, London, UK

Neil Soneji BSc Final year medical student, Imperial College London, London, UK

Asil Tahir BSc Final year medical student, Barts and The London School of Medicine and Dentistry, London, UK

Introduction to *Secrets of Success*

It is now over 16 years since we first met at medical school, united by a passion for education and a desire to excel in our medical careers. During this time, we have been working together and have actively designed and delivered numerous products to facilitate the development of medical students and junior doctors.

The 'Secrets of Success' series has been designed in order to address the void in the development of pre-medical students, medical students and junior doctors. Our aim is to provide mentorship and comprehensive guidance to facilitate success through a portfolio of innovative products that reflect our enthusiasm, energy and unique style. We hope that you and your future careers can benefit from the knowledge of our own experiences. All too often, we are told to aim to achieve 'competence' in medicine. Our philosophy is to never settle for anything less than 'excellence' and being the best that you can possibly be!

This series of books embodies this philosophy. This instalment is aimed at helping you get into medical school, which we hope will be the first step towards a long and successful career in medicine.

Marc A Gladman and Manoj Ramachandran
Series Editors

Preface

This book is suitable for anyone considering a career in medicine, from GCSE students to university graduates to workers looking for a career change. It will help you enhance your application as well as decide whether or not a career in medicine is right for you. You can also use it as a reference guide when preparing for various stages of the application process.

Applying to medical school has become increasingly competitive but, at the same time, the doors have been unlocked for many applicants for whom the career would have been unthinkable in the past. There are improved opportunities for graduates, including accelerated 4-year programmes, there are more options for mature candidates, and there are a handful of extended programmes for gifted students from disadvantaged backgrounds.

We aim to give you ideas and guidance on how to bring out the best in yourself as a future doctor in order to secure the place you deserve at medical school. We have come to realize that the rigid and regimented advice that many continue to receive can be uninspiring and can limit bright applicants to monotony and subsequent disappointment. By helping you understand how to make the most out of everything you do, we hope you will feel empowered to control your preparation and succeed. We focus on how you can use your initiative, work with other students, reflect on your achievements and maximize your performance at each hurdle of the admissions process.

Why do we think these methods will work? It is because they will make you better medical students and doctors and, ultimately, that's what medical schools are looking for.

If you have any feedback, questions or suggestions, please let us know (viyaasan@hotmail.com).

Good luck!

VM, MAG, MR

Acknowledgements

We are grateful to the following staff, students and graduates of Barts & The London School of Medicine & Dentistry for their willing help, enthusiastic ideas and valued insight:

Dr Cathy Baker, Dr Shin Hann Chia, Nader Ibrahim, Mansum Ng, Christine Sofianos and David Tai.

We are also grateful to Sarah Vasey and Sarah Ogden at RSM Press for their patience, support and guidance throughout this project.

VM:
I would like to thank my good friend Metin Devrim Yalçin for his steadfast encouragement, and my degree supervisors Dr Steve Harwood and Dr Martin Carrier for their kind support at the time of writing.

This book is dedicated to my father.

Key to icons

 Top Tip

 Question

 Facts and Figures

 Danger

 Money

1 Taking the plunge

Making the decision to study medicine should be carefully thought out and thoroughly explored. The earlier that you start this preparation process the better, as this will give you the best opportunity to gain the necessary experiences and get yourself into the right frame of mind for the career.

Medical students may find acclimatizing to medical school difficult because of differences in expectation, and lack of motivation, inspiration and enjoyment of the work. For this reason, the schools are keen to assess how much thought you have put into making this career choice and how much effort you have made in finding out more about it.

At the same time, the demand for entry continues to grow, making the selection process for medical schools increasingly challenging. Nearly all courses now require an admissions test, which is used in collaboration with your previous academic performance, your predicted future performance, your personal statement, your reference and your interview in a variety of ways to offer places to a fraction of the applicants. It is therefore vital that you stand out among this strong crowd by optimizing your performance in every area.

In this book, we offer you some ideas as to how you can do this and ensure that you put yourself in a strong position. However, you should make of it what you will and tailor your preparations to suit you. Going through the motions can be tedious, so you should be creative, take interest in what you need to do and go for it your way. There is no fixed formula for success, but taking the initiative and being able to articulate your experiences in an honest and engaging way will come through strongly and fill you with a genuine sense of pride and motivation.

Be on the ball

It is important to be aware of what is going on around you. This involves trying to get to the bottom of what admissions panels want to see and how you are going to be able to show this to them. If there are any weaknesses in your application that cannot be worked on, you need to look for the right opportunities around them. Get in touch with the medical schools in which you are interested and find out for certain how much that weakness is going to cost you in relation to an alternative medical school.

There are many Internet forums where applicants are able to discuss the application process, including www.admissionsforum. net and www.newmediamedicine.com/forum. If there is anything in particular that you need to know but cannot find, these are good places to start, as there will be other applicants, medical students and doctors who have already got in who can point you in the right direction.

Enjoy the process

Try to enjoy the process of preparing for medicine – if you don't, you need to think about preparing in different ways or it may be that the career is not for you. Immerse yourself in work experience placements and voluntary work so that you can appreciate the minute details of the career and impress the people around you who will respect you and be willing to help.

Explore the subject and make the most of it! Medicine is much more than the finest anatomical details or the precise mechanisms of every drug, particularly at the stage that you are at. It is also about the relationship between doctors and patients within a wider social, political and economic context. It is full of unique ethical dilemmas and controversies, as well as fascinating discoveries and innovations. There is so much out there to find out about and discuss with others, and it will play a role in shaping your personal and professional development through your values and inspirations.

Work with others

We would also recommend that you work with other students who are applying. This means that you can motivate each other, discuss issues as a group to explore your own understanding and share the responsibilities for preparations among yourselves (see Chapter 5). In many walks of life, bringing out the best in you involves working with other people by identifying common goals and moving towards them.

You should also keep in touch with people whom you meet along the way, such as the students who show you around a medical school at an open day, junior doctors from your work experience placement and admissions officers. Many people are happy to help you if they can see your honest approach and your dedication.

 Ensure that you have a sensible email address that you can use for professional correspondence. It is best to use an address that incorporates your name, as many college or university accounts do. Otherwise, a Googlemail or Hotmail account will do.

Keep a portfolio

We would recommend that you get started on putting together a presentable portfolio of **all** your experiences and achievements. With all the experience that you have, you should try to obtain a letter of reference detailing your achievements and the personal qualities that you have shown.

You may also keep any reflective writing that you have done. Such material is often used by medical schools to reinforce students' experiences. This may be done each day after your work experience placements or voluntary work, in the form of a diary or as a summary of an article that you have read. These reflections are useful for consolidating your understanding and refreshing your memory closer to interviews. You may also wish to include any good pieces of work that you have done, particularly if they are of relevance to medicine, including PowerPoint slides of any presentations that you have given to your peers.

Your portfolio should be presented to your UCAS referee; they will be impressed by your organization and commitment, as well as your achievements and references. This will be reflected positively in your UCAS reference.

Stay committed to your studies

You need to stay on top of your work at all times. Getting into medicine requires top grades and there is little margin for error. It is vital that you stay organized and build all of your additional activities around your work.

If you see yourself slipping, it is important to acknowledge this, identify why and try to sort it out as soon as possible. By taking an interest in your work, there is a good chance that you will appreciate what you are learning better and see big improvements. Try to keep good relationships with your teachers and lecturers, as they will feed back positively to your UCAS referee and be willing to help you as much as they can. You can also find added motivation by working with other students to utilize each other's strengths positively as a group.

2 Do you really want to become a doctor?

Before you commit yourself to a career in medicine, ensure that you are well acquainted with the realities of the profession. Work experience, speaking to doctors and medical students, and reading online resources should all be part of your preparation. You are about to make a very important decision and it is not something that you would want to get wrong! In this chapter, we introduce you to the ins and outs of a medical career.

Be warned that much of this may seem complicated, but have a read through and try to get the gist of it. If you aren't fazed by what's ahead, you should explore the career further through work experience.

The career path

A career in medicine can be divided into three parts:

1. Medical student (4–6 years)
2. Junior doctor (5 or more years)
3. Hospital specialist (consultant) or general practitioner (GP).

Each stage has its hoops and hurdles that you need to overcome in order to progress. You should also be committed to lifelong learning.

Medical student

To practise as a doctor, you must have a degree in medicine, which conventionally lasts 5 years in the UK. Usually, the course is divided into pre-clinical and clinical phases, although this distinction is becoming increasingly blurred.

The pre-clinical phase takes up the first 2 years. Here students are taught the basic sciences behind medicine. The main areas of study are the structure and function of the body (anatomy and physiology), the body in disease (pathology) and how drugs work (pharmacology). Most medical schools now have an integrated curriculum, where these subjects are taught in combination for each body system (e.g. the cardiovascular system). Teaching can take the form of lectures, tutorials, problem-based learning (PBL), laboratory sessions and computer-assisted learning (CAL), with varying emphasis depending on the medical school. Increasingly, courses are introducing clinical teaching early, with visits to hospitals or general practices.

During the clinical phase, students spend most of their time in hospitals, where they learn how different diseases present in patients. Each hospital will have a teaching programme run by its doctors, and students learn how to clerk a patient's medical history, conduct examinations and perform basic practical procedures (such as taking blood and putting in cannulae). They are encouraged to get fully involved and work closely with junior doctors as a member of the team (known as the 'firm'). Students can be placed in firms in both teaching hospitals (usually located close to the medical school) and district general hospitals (DGHs). Students are sometimes sent to DGHs located far from the medical school and they are usually provided with on-site accommodation while they are there. If not, there can be some daily long hauls!

Another increasingly important feature of medical courses is student-selected components (SSCs). These are modules that take place in each year, which students can either choose from a list or self-organize. These give students the opportunity to pursue particular interests in greater depth, learn more about an area to which they haven't had much exposure or work on aspects that they feel they need to improve. They often get closer attention from supervisors and may be able to carry out audits (see Chapter 11) or short research projects that can enhance their CV.

In addition to the basic medical course, it is also possible to gain an intercalated degree. This is an additional bachelor's degree in a subject of interest, taken during an extra year. (The exception to this is the University of Nottingham, where students graduate with a BMedSci degree within the 5-year programme.) At a few medical schools, it is compulsory, but at most it is optional. The range of subjects on offer can vary, and it is sometimes possible to transfer to a different medical school if a course that a student is keen on is not offered at his or her own institution. Most intercalated degrees involve a research project that the student will need to write up in a dissertation. With some luck and hard work, they are sometimes able to publish their findings in a medical journal or present it at a national or international conference.

Junior doctor

Since 2005, following an initiative called Modernising Medical Careers (MMC), the career path for junior doctors has changed significantly. The overall aims of MMC were to increase the number of consultants (fully trained senior doctors) and to make training for junior doctors more streamlined.

As a result of some serious hiccups, MMC has come under a lot of high-profile criticism. Many doctors and students have realized that you need to make up your mind about where you want your career to head very early on, and that you need to get ready for some serious competition to get there. This has led to disillusionment for a few, with some doctors deciding to leave and train abroad instead. In January 2008, Professor Sir John Tooke, Dean of Peninsula Medical School, published an Inquiry into MMC (commonly referred to as the Tooke Report). The Report identified the inefficiencies and the failings of the initiative and proposed significant changes, which are slowly being implemented.

The evolution of junior doctors' training from the past to the present to the future is shown in Figure 2.1.

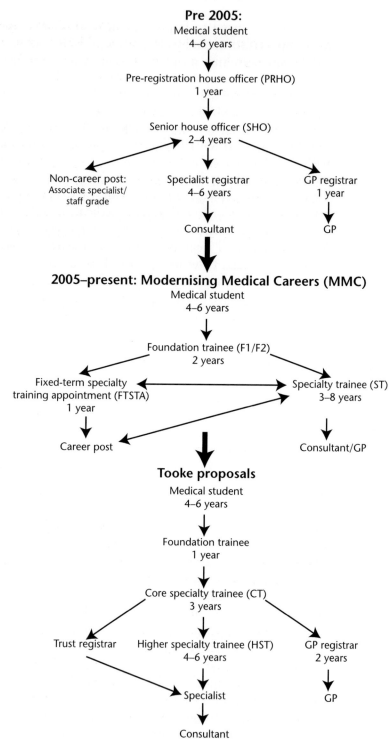

Figure 2.1 Past, present and future career pathways for doctors.

Under the old system, new medical graduates spent 1 year as a pre-registration house officer (PRHO) followed by an indefinite period as a senior house office (SHO). After this, doctors applied for registrar positions, which began the training process in a particular specialty. In order to improve this process and avoid wasted SHO years, MMC created the Foundation Programme to ensure that all UK medical graduates were of a suitable standard by the time they applied to specialty training. However, among the recommendations of the Tooke Report, the Foundation Programme is to be reduced to 1 year, after which doctors undertake core specialty training (CT). After the end of CT, doctors will move to higher specialty training (HST). This is similar to the recent 'uncoupling' of several specialty training programmes.

Training is provided by regional 'foundation schools' and 'deaneries' through their local NHS trusts. Junior doctor training is divided into two stages:

1. Foundation Training: 2 years
2. GP/Specialist Training: 3–8 years.

Foundation training

www.foundationprogramme.nhs.uk

Foundation training involves 2 years of work, which is mostly based in hospitals. The first year is called Foundation Year 1 (F1) and the second year F2. Most doctors spend 4-month stints in different departments for 2 years. Most F1 jobs are in general medicine and general surgery, whereas at F2 there are greater opportunities to experience general practice and accident and emergency, as well as other specialties.

Almost all medical graduates get a job in foundation training. The current application process is national and takes the form of a computer-based questionnaire called the 'Foundation Programme Application Service'. This is often referred to by doctors and medical students as 'MTAS' after the 'Medical Training Application Service' which was abandoned in 2007. Applicants are scored based on their 'white space' responses (which relate to their academic and non-academic experiences), their ranking at medical school and any additional educational achievements (previous/intercalated degrees, publications and presentations). Applicants must list in order of preference the foundation schools in which they want to train and subsequently the rotations at the various hospitals that they want to do. Each applicant is matched to a job based on their score.

However, from 2010, this process is due to change. There is currently an uncertainty with regards to its legality, and also question marks over the principle of giving the highest-scoring applicants priority over where they want to work. The concern is that this may create a geographical disparity in the quality of foundation doctors, which potentially disadvantages patients in less attractive regions and hospitals. A national exam, structured interviews and portfolio assessment are potential alternatives that are being considered.

Specialty/GP training

www.mmc.nhs.uk

During F2, doctors apply for specialty training (ST) or general practice specialty training (GPST) posts. GPST lasts for 3 years, whereas ST, depending on the specialty chosen, can take up to 8 years. ST doctors are assessed based on their competencies, and must achieve minimum requirements for their Record of In-Training Assessment (RITA) in order to progress each year.

Some hospital specialties have now 'uncoupled' programmes, which means that trainees receive 'core training' for 2 or 3 years, after which they have to compete again for 'higher specialty training'. In others, they receive 'run-through training' which means that they do not have to compete any further. The traditional job title of SHO continues to be used to describe core trainees or those in their first 2–3 years of ST, while the title of registrar is given thereafter.

If you thought that you would be done with exams at university, think again! The training programmes are regulated by 'Colleges', such as the Royal Colleges of Physicians, Surgeons, and Obstetricians and Gynaecologists. In addition to the core competencies that need to be demonstrated on the job, these Colleges also set exams for postgraduate diplomas, which must be passed in order to be awarded membership of the College. To be a physician, for instance, you need to be a Member of the Royal College of Physicians (MRCP). These exams are expensive and difficult, with many doctors needing to repeat them before they pass.

Many doctors also take time out to study for a higher degree such as an MD (Doctor of Medicine) or PhD (Doctor of Philosophy) (see Academic medicine below). Although this elongates the training period, these degrees enhance CVs and give the doctors the opportunity to complete a formal period of research, culminating in a thesis. They publish work in medical journals and have the opportunity to give international presentations, which raise their profile within their chosen field.

Unsurprisingly, the ST application process is much more complicated and competitive than for F1. There are a limited number of posts within each specialty around the country. For most specialties, there is no centralized national application process, so doctors need to look for training positions in individual deaneries and apply to them. The deaneries then short list for interviews before making offers. On successfully obtaining a training post, doctors are given a National Training Number (NTN).

Those who do not get in at this stage can apply for a Fixed-Term Specialty Training Appointment (FTSTA), where, for a year, they train alongside ST, but need to reapply for ST to progress further.

The different specialties

The career options for a doctor are vast, but, because of MMC, the decision to specialize is forced upon the doctor quite early on. It is important to make the most of the exposure gained at medical school to get a flavour of everything so as not to make the wrong career decision.

General practice

General practice is the largest specialty in medicine. General practitioners (GPs) generally come together in partnerships to acquire practices from primary care trusts (PCTs), which are run as small businesses. The 'partners' are responsible for how the practice should spend its allocated money from the PCT, including employing staff such as receptionists, secretaries and nurses, as well as 'salaried GPs'. Following the General Medical Services (GMS) contract in 2004, practices have been paid by the NHS based on their performance in the 'Quality Outcomes Framework' (QOF), an incentive scheme measuring how well they implement best practice guidelines.

GPs are the gatekeepers of the NHS, and will often need to refer their patients on for specialist help. Although they are required to have a broad knowledge base, they are increasingly expected to have special interests of their own in which they can run clinics. For instance, a GP with an interest in dermatology may run a clinic where he or she sees skin problems and performs minor procedures.

The GMS contract made general practice a more attractive specialty, although partners are required to have a degree of business acumen. Unsurprisingly, it has become increasingly difficult to find partnership opportunities and many GPs have had to work indefinitely in salaried posts until the right opportunity comes along. PCTs are also becoming increasingly open to giving practices to private companies that they feel have more expertise in running a business. These companies in turn recruit salaried GPs and other staff to provide patient care.

As well as working in community-based practices, GPs can also work in an accident and emergency department (A&E). Often, there will be a GP service attached to the department to handle minor cases. They can also provide out-of-hours care if necessary to patients in their homes via NHS Direct.

We would strongly advise you to arrange work experience at a local practice to find out more about this important area of the NHS.

Training

Some F2 doctors will work in general practice for 4 months, but this is not essential for graduates determined to pursue this career. GPST lasts for 3 years, although it is anticipated that this will be extended to 5 years in the near future. Much of this time is spent as a hospital SHO in fields such as obstetrics and gynaecology (O&G) and paediatrics, before spending 1 year working as a GP registrar. It is essential for trainees to obtain the MRCGP (Membership of the Royal College of General Practitioners) before they can work independently. They are also advised to obtain additional postgraduate diplomas such as the DRCOG (Diploma of the Royal College of Obstetricians and Gynaecologists) or DCH (Diploma in Child Health) in areas of specialist interest. Hospital specialists can move into general practice with reasonable ease should they have a change of heart, although it is more difficult to go the other way.

Hospital specialties

Medicine

Medicine is a broad term covering many non-surgical specialties. Consultants who practise medicine are known as physicians. In addition to providing specialist care, 'general physicians' are also required to provide general medical care. This is because hospitals will rotate the physician 'on take' on a rota basis and, while the physician is 'on take', they are responsible for every patient admitted from A&E or from their GP with a medical problem. They may subsequently refer the patient to the relevant specialist, but this may not be necessary if the problem remains within the expertise of the general physician.

It is for this reason, and the fact that many patients have illnesses involving a variety of body systems, that physicians need to have a strong general medical knowledge, particularly of acute problems. ST therefore begins with 2 years of core medical training (CMT) or the acute care common stem (ACCS) before trainees reapply at ST3 for training in a particular medical specialty. The main medical specialties, as well as a few of the smaller ones, are as follows.

General medicine

1. Acute medicine (early management of medical problems)
2. Cardiology (heart)
3. Care of the elderly
4. Endocrinology and diabetes (hormones)
5. Gastroenterology (digestive system)
6. Infectious diseases
7. Neurology (nervous system)
8. Renal medicine (kidneys)
9. Respiratory medicine (lungs).

Medical specialties

1. Clinical genetics (diagnosis and counselling of patients with genetic disorders)
2. Clinical pharmacology and therapeutics (use of drugs)
3. Dermatology (skin)
4. Genitourinary medicine (GUM) (sexual health)
5. Haematology (blood)
6. Medical ophthalmology (vision)
7. Oncology (cancer)
8. Palliative medicine (symptom relief/improving quality of life in complex or terminal diseases)
9. Rheumatology (joints and connective tissue diseases)
10. Sports and exercise medicine
11. Tropical medicine.

The general medical consultants tend to have the most hospital inpatients and are therefore the ones who are usually involved in general medical rotas. Physicians from the other medical specialties will usually conduct outpatient clinics and visit a few inpatients, often in liaison with general physicians. These jobs tend to have a more relaxed schedule out of hours, although they require a great depth of knowledge.

During foundation training, every doctor will have exposure to general medicine and will be required to work on call or on an acute medicine rotation. Those who choose to specialize in general medicine will have a large amount of contact with acutely unwell patients. Those in higher ST (ST3 upwards) will be working as 'medical registrars'. When on call, the medical registrar is the first point of contact for GPs and A&E doctors should they want to admit a patient. They need to visit many patients all over the hospital, delegate tasks to juniors and liaise with a variety of departments. These responsibilities are accentuated out of hours and the medical registrar on call effectively runs the hospital at night and on weekends. Some find this an enviable position, whereas others find it daunting, but these experiences make them good consultant physicians further down the career pathway.

Consultant physicians lead outpatient clinics, undertake ward rounds and have many administrative duties. They are also responsible for supervising the training of junior doctors and medical students. When they are on take, they usually carry on with their normal jobs, but, at the end of the take, they perform a ward round where they see all the patients who have been admitted under their care and decide on what to do next with each of them.

In many specialist centres, cardiologists have their own on-call rota, where a special team sees only heart-related admissions. Cardiologists are also able to venture into the realm of minimally invasive interventional procedures such as angioplasties and pacemaker insertions. Some specialist units perform angioplasties on patients who come in after heart attacks, and so an on-call interventional cardiologist needs to be available at all times.

Similar to interventional cardiologists, most gastroenterologists are now skilled in endoscopy, and some respiratory physicians have special interests in bronchoscopy. These aspects are appealing to those who prefer medicine to surgery but would also like some hands-on work.

Training

Following foundation training, applicants can go through either CMT or ACCS, both of which are 2-year programmes. At the end of these, trainees can apply for ST3 posts in any medical specialty, although those who entered ACCS also have the options of anaesthetics and emergency medicine (see below). As registrar training posts are competed for, CMT and ACCS trainees are advised to complete the MRCP by the time that they apply.

Paediatric medicine

www.rcpch.ac.uk/doc.aspx?id_Resource2160

In the latter half of the twentieth century, paediatric medicine and child health emerged as a separate medical specialty. Paediatricians exclusively treat children and in most hospitals are generalists who look after all non-surgical aspects of the ill child. However, in teaching hospitals and specialist children's hospitals, there are almost as many subspecialties as there are in adults, including gastroenterology, cardiology and neurology. Unlike adult physicians, consultant paediatricians are regularly called in out of hours to deal with difficult cases. Paediatrics often deals with very different diseases to those found in adults and communication is a different ballgame altogether, as information needs to be obtained from both children (when possible) and parents. Crying children can also be difficult to examine and perform investigations on, so opportunism and powers of negotiation and distraction are essential.

A distinct branch of paediatrics is neonatology. These doctors look after unwell newborns (e.g. premature births) who may require intensive care. The specialty involves a lot of intricate hands-on work and requires a lot of communication with distressed parents, including mothers who may have gone through difficult labours. In DGHs, the general paediatrician may be required to cover the neonatal unit when on call, although neonatology services are increasingly being provided by specialist centres.

There are also many community paediatricians. These doctors work in specialist community centres and look after children with developmental problems and disabilities (e.g. Down's syndrome or deafness). Their responsibilities are to optimize the wellbeing of these children in their everyday lives by working with the multidisciplinary team (e.g. physiotherapists) and schools. Some are also involved in child protection services in abuse cases.

Training

Unlike adult medical training, paediatric training is run through, so there is no need for SHOs to reapply for registrar posts. Training lasts for 5 years, during which time trainees need to obtain the MRCPCH (Membership of the Royal College of Paediatrics and Child Health).

Surgery

www.rcseng.ac.uk/career/surgical-specialties

Surgeons treat patients with operative procedures, although their greatest responsibility is in evaluating who should and shouldn't be operated on. Interestingly, it is a professional tradition in Britain for surgeons to abandon the title 'doctor' and be known as 'mister' or 'miss', although, due to public confusion, there have recently been calls for this practice to end. This originates from mediaeval Europe, where surgery was performed by barber surgeons and not qualified doctors.

The main surgical specialties are as follows.

General surgery

1. Breast
2. Colorectal (large bowel, rectum and anus)
3. Endocrine (glands, especially thyroid and adrenal)
4. Hepato pancreato biliary (HPB) (liver pancreas and gallbladder)
5. Transplantation (usually kidney and liver)
6. Upper gastrointestinal (oesophagus and stomach)
7. Vascular (blood vessels).

Surgical specialties

1. Cardiothoracic surgery (heart, lung, aorta and oesophagus)
2. Ear, nose and throat (ENT) (includes head and neck cancer surgery)
3. Neurosurgery (brain and spinal cord)
4. Ophthalmology (vision)
5. Oral and maxillofacial surgery (mouth, jaws, face and neck)
6. Paediatric surgery (general surgery in children)

7. Plastic surgery and burns (reconstruction)
8. Trauma and orthopaedics (musculoskeletal diseases and fractures)
9. Urology (urinary tract and male genital tract).

As with general physicians, general surgeons have an area of expertise, as well as a breadth of knowledge. When on call, they are usually required to carry out emergency abdominal surgery for problems such as acute appendicitis or urgent hernia repair. When not on call, they undertake elective cases in their specialized area, which are planned ahead (e.g. a colorectal surgeon may remove a cancerous portion of bowel). In some centres, vascular surgery has a separate on-call service, as patients may present in life-threatening states that require experienced hands. Laparoscopic (keyhole) techniques have revolutionized abdominal surgery in that they offer better outcomes and faster recovery. As a result, many surgeons have decided to focus their expertise on these methods.

The surgical specialties all have on-call responsibilities of their own, although these services may not be offered by all hospitals. Most evening and weekend on-call duties, including emergency operations, are carried out by trainees, with the on-call consultant rarely being called in out of hours.

Paediatric surgeons exclusively treat babies, children and teenagers, although they mostly deal with abdominal problems. A recent development is antenatal surgery, in which fetuses may be operated on inside the mother's womb. The other specialties also have paediatric branches in which surgeons treat children's diseases of their anatomical area of expertise (e.g. a paediatric orthopaedic surgeon treats congenital and developmental bone and joint problems in children).

Training

All foundation trainees spend some time in surgery. When it comes to ST, neurosurgery (8 years) and ophthalmology (7 years) have separate run-through training paths, which begin at ST1 and do not require re-application further down the line. Trainees looking for a career in general surgery and the other surgical specialties must undergo 2 years of basic surgical training (BST) before competing for higher surgical training (HST) in their chosen specialty at ST3 level. Those undergoing BST are known as surgical SHOs and are expected to complete their MRCS (Membership of the Royal College of Surgeons). Those undergoing HST are known as surgical registrars. HST lasts a further 5 or 6 years, depending on the specialty, during which time trainees complete their FRCS (Fellowship of the Royal College of Surgeons). Throughout surgical training, trainees keep a logbook of their experiences and they need to fulfil predetermined requirements in order to progress.

Doctors wishing to go into oral and maxillofacial surgery are required to qualify in dentistry as well as medicine before they can embark on HST. As it is possible to carry on earning part time as a dentist or oral surgeon while studying medicine, it is usually dental graduates who decide to go into this field, although there are an increasing number of doctors taking the alternative route. Qualified dentists may do special accelerated 3-year medical degrees. After qualifying in medicine, these doctors must also do foundation training and BST before applying for HST programmes in oral and maxillofacial surgery.

Obstetrics and gynaecology (O&G)

O&G is effectively a combination of two specialties dealing with women's health. Obstetrics is the care of pregnant women, whereas gynaecology deals with diseases of the female genital tract. O&G is seen as being a combination of both medicine and surgery. Consultants usually specialize further in fetal medicine, gynaecological oncology, urogynaecology, sexual health or reproductive medicine. Reproductive specialists use technology to improve fertility.

Both obstetrics and gynaecology usually have separate on-call rotas, which means that there can be a lot of out-of-hours work involved. Given the nature of childbirth, obstetrics can be particularly unpredictable and consultants often need to be called in. There is also a higher level of litigation involved in O&G compared with other specialties.

Training

O&G training is a 7-year run-through programme. By the end, trainees must have obtained the MRCOG. Some will also choose to obtain the MRCS.

Anaesthesia

Anaesthetists are physicians who are responsible for looking after patients during surgery, as well as running intensive care departments and providing pain management services. They are therefore looking after patients in their most sick and vulnerable states, and often need to act quickly to save those who are deteriorating. As part of surgical care, anaesthetists assess patients before operations, put them to sleep or give them a regional anaesthetic, and then monitor their wellbeing throughout the procedure. Anaesthetists are also required in obstetric teams, providing pain relief to mothers during childbirth, and are also often a part of cardiac arrest crash teams. There are more anaesthetists in hospitals than any other specialty.

Training

Anaesthetic trainees may go through the 7-year anaesthetic programme or the 8-year programme with ACCS. If they choose the ACCS path, they subsequently join the anaesthetic programme at ST2. During training, they need to complete the FRCA (Fellowship of the Royal College of Anaesthetists) before they can practise as consultants. FRCA Part 1 must be completed by ST2 and FRCA Part 2 by ST4.

Emergency medicine

Emergency physicians work in A&E, where they are required to deal with the variety of patients who come through the door. Some may require resuscitation after serious trauma, some may be very unstable, and some may have minor injuries and require stitching. Working in A&E is very different to working in other hospital departments and can be faster paced and pressured. As a result of government legislation, all patients must be discharged or referred to another department within 4 hours of coming through the door. The doctors also work shifts – often at nights and weekends. The only subspecialty of emergency medicine is paediatric emergency medicine, although most trainees and consultants spend some time in this part of the department.

Training

Many F2 doctors spend 3–6 months in A&E. Those wanting to pursue a career in emergency medicine need to do ACCS as well as ST3 in A&E. By the end of this, they need to have obtained an MCEM (Membership of the College of Emergency Medicine) or an equivalent diploma, as well as completed three advanced life support (ALS) courses before competing again for ST4 posts. Registrar training (ST4–6) also lasts 3 years, and so the total training time is 6 years. By the end of this, they must have completed FCEM. Some trainees may wish to extend their training in order to obtain accreditation in both emergency medicine and intensive care medicine.

Psychiatry

*www.rcpsych.ac.uk/training/careersinpsychiatry/
careerinfoforschoolleavers.aspx*

Psychiatry is another very large specialty. It is very different to other branches of medicine. Psychiatrists usually work both in hospital mental health units and in the community, and there are several different areas of interest, including general adult psychiatry, old age psychiatry, child and adolescent psychiatry, substance misuse, forensic psychiatry, liaison psychiatry, and learning disabilities.

Psychiatrists usually work in large teams with social workers, community psychiatric nurses and psychologists. The old lunatic asylums are long gone as patients are kept as inpatients only when necessary and the emphasis is placed on looking after them in the community. Even within the hospital ward, patients are given independent rooms and are encouraged to tend to their daily activities.

The specialty relies heavily on strong communication skills, as psychiatrists need to obtain long and detailed histories from their patients and examine their mental state through a series of questions. They are also unique in that they are legally approved by the Mental Health Act to 'section' patients (detain under their care acutely unwell patients without their consent). On-call duties are less intense than in other specialties, even for trainees, because there are few emergencies, and many are dealt with initially by nurses.

Training

ST lasts for 6 years, although there is another round of competitive entry for ST4. Trainees need to obtain MRCPsych (Member of the Royal College of Psychiatrists).

Radiology

As a result of advances in imaging techniques such as computed tomography (CT) and magnetic resonance imaging (MRI), radiology has become one of the most attractive specialties. While traditionally radiologists used imaging for diagnosis, they are increasingly using their expertise to treat patients by imaging-assisted, minimally invasive methods, gulping up work that was once performed by surgeons, as well as treating patients who previously would have been deemed unsuitable for treatment. This area of the specialty is called 'interventional radiology'.

The diagnostic skills of radiologists are frequently called upon by most other specialists and each department usually holds regular radiology meetings, meaning that radiologists must have a good eye for detail and strong communications skills. They must also have an excellent knowledge of anatomy.

Training

Clinical radiology training is run through and lasts 5 years. Trainees are required to obtain the FRCR (Fellowship of the Royal College of Radiologists), although some also obtain diplomas from other colleges such as the MRCS.

Academic opportunities

The quest for knowledge in all medical fields is greater than ever and universities are driven by both the public and the private sectors to carry out research. Medical research can broadly take one of three forms:

1. Laboratory research: to understand disease processes at a cellular and molecular level and discover new disease markers or therapeutic targets and agents
2. Clinical research: to understand the course of a disease in patients as well as measure the effectiveness of novel diagnostic methods and therapies
3. Epidemiological research: to understand public health issues and identify the causes of diseases.

As it is such an effective way of enhancing their professional reputation, many doctors at some point in their careers undertake research. The first opportunity to do so is as a student. This may be done voluntarily or by undertaking an intercalated degree during the undergraduate medical course. During intercalated degree courses, students are introduced to basic research methods and often work on a supervised research project that contributes to a larger piece of work.

As part of measures to fast-track doctors into an academic career, a separate career path called Integrated Academic Training (a.k.a. the Walport Pathway) has been created that runs parallel to the conventional MMC path. It is, however, possible to crossover between the two paths at the different entry points.

There are a few academic programmes incorporated into foundation training in each foundation school that are linked to the local universities. Recruitment for these programmes takes place before the conventional application process and students must apply directly to foundation schools, much like the ST application. The foundation schools usually short list candidates for interviews. Students who are interested in entering academic foundation programmes are encouraged to do intercalated degrees and voluntary research during their undergraduate studies, which they should aim to publish and present at conferences. Academic foundation trainees complete F1 similar to everyone else, but are given protected time at F2 to undertake some research in addition to their clinical work.

There are similar ST programmes available known as Academic Clinical Fellowships (ACFs) and subsequently Clinical Lectureships (CLs). There are approximately 250 ACF programmes available each year. These last for 3 years and Fellows spend three-quarters of their time in clinical training and a quarter doing research. At the end of this, Fellows receive a higher degree such as a PhD. Those with higher degrees, as well as an NTN, are able to apply for CLs. These take place towards the end of ST and last for up to 4 years. During this time, lecturers spend half their time on clinical duties and the other half undertaking postdoctoral research.

If doctors do not get onto an ACF programme, they are still able to undertake higher degree courses, albeit at the expense of time and earnings. As these are not integrated, they need to take time out of ST to complete them. Programmes for an MD usually last 1 year, whereas a PhD will take at least 3 years. It is also often possible to undertake research (usually no longer than a year) within the conventional ST training path at the latter stages.

It is hoped that these fast-tracked academics will become the professors of the future. Some professors are clinicians who are employed by both a university and an NHS trust. They are leading scientists responsible for conducting advanced research and supervising junior investigators, as well as senior clinicians with a high level of professional respect (often being the head of a department). Other professors abandon their clinical work and focus exclusively on their academic commitments. Other consultants with academic commitments who are not professors usually hold senior lecturer or reader positions at a university. Some universities have followed other countries in referring to these consultants as associate professors.

In addition to research programmes, there are a few educational academic programmes, in which trainees have formal teaching committments and undertake research in areas of medical education such as curriculum design. However, it should be remembered that medical teaching is not exclusive to educationalists and that all doctors are expected to supervise and teach students, colleagues and allied health-care professionals both formally and informally. The aim of these programmes is to encourage doctors to improve the overall delivery of medical education.

Academic doctors aim to publish their research in medical journals and present them at international conferences. Articles are reviewed by an editorial board and peer experts in the field of research, before being accepted or rejected for publication. There is a hierarchy of prestige associated with journals, with some having a greater impact than others. Publications and presentations form an important part of a doctor's CV at all levels and, the greater the impact, the stronger the CV. In addition to research, doctors can also write review papers or commentaries in which the existing medical literature is put together and analysed. It is worthwhile having a look at a journal such as the *British Medical Journal*, where there are a few original research papers and review papers published each week.

The competitiveness

Even after getting into medical school, there is a lot of competition ahead. This is not unlike many other professions. Competition at foundation training is for places at a particular foundation school, and subsequently for jobs within that school. However, the Department of Health is keen that every medical graduate has a place in foundation training.

Competition starts to get tough at ST level, where it can be difficult to get the training programme that you want in your preferred deanery. With the exception of those specialties that operate on national recruitment, each deanery has the autonomy to choose its trainees. It is for this reason that you need to have a strong portfolio of your achievements and experiences, as well as good insight into what they are interested in, to succeed at this level.

The competition ratios from 2008 are shown in Table 2.1 to give an idea of how competitive each specialty is. It should be

Table 2.1 Competition ratios for 2008

Training programme	Applications per post
Paediatric surgery	40
Clinical radiology	33
Cardiothoracic surgery	23
Chemical pathology	23
Plastic surgery	23
Medical microbiology and virology	22
ACCS	19
General surgery	19
Ophthalmology	19
Trauma and orthopaedic surgery	15
Urology	15
ENT	14
Oral and maxillofacial surgery	13
BST	12
Anaesthesia	9
CMT	9
Psychiatry	9
General adult psychiatry	7
Cleft lip and palate surgery	6
O&G	6
Public health	6
Histopathology	5
Neurosurgery	5
Paediatrics	4
General practice	3

ACCS, acute care common stem; BST, basic surgical training; CMT, core medical training; ENT, ear, nose and throat; O&G, obstetrics and gynaecology.

remembered that these ratios usually vary year on year and between different deaneries.

Keeping up with the competition requires commitment, dedication and planning, and what you should do at medical school is not too different from what we would advise you to do to get *into* medical school. You should aim to do well academically, think about where you want your career to go, and, when possible, organize placements, audits or research projects in areas of interest, be involved in non-academic activities that will give you valuable skills, and keep up to date with developments in medicine and training. The last detail is sometimes ignored even by bright and high-flying students, but it can be the most important because it has an uncanny power of motivation for all the other areas.

Flexible training

It is possible for doctors to undergo their training part time over a longer period. They can cut up to 50% of their working week, which can be useful for doctors who want to spend more time with their families. Although this is becoming increasingly viable as there are initiatives to increase the number of doctors who take up this option, those who do so need to do some running around and organizing to ensure that their deanery and NHS trust are happy with the arrangements and that it is legitimate from a training perspective.

Pregnant women and new mothers returning to work are entitled to change their hours and be exempt from out-of-hours work, although they need to ensure that their deanery approves this as part of their training.

The cost of becoming a doctor

Medicine is a comparatively expensive degree for most British students. Under the new 'top-up fees' system, students pay £3145 a year (and rising) in fees for the first 4 years of the course, which is paid for by a Fee Loan. It is likely that this cap will soon be increased to give universities more freedom to charge their own fees. The Fee Loan needs to be paid off when you start working in addition to a Maintenance Loan (which covers living costs based on your parents' income). After the fourth year of the course, fees are paid for by the NHS.

However, there are exceptions to this rule:

1. Scottish residents and residents from EU countries other than England, Wales or Northern Ireland pay no tuition fees if they attend a Scottish medical school

2. Welsh residents and residents from EU countries other than England, Scotland or Northern Ireland pay a reduced rate of £1250 if they attend a Welsh medical school.

The Maintenance Loan is means tested each year and ranges from £2763 for students living at home outside London to £4988 for those living away from home in London. You may also be eligible for an additional Maintenance Grant of up to £2906 per year, which is means tested and does not have to be paid back. Depending on your circumstances you could finish your degree in up to £40 000 of debt to the Student Loan Company, which rises with inflation.

In addition to the Student Loan, a student bank account gives you access to an interest-free overdraft of up to £2000 for the duration of your study. Those studying in England who receive the maximum student loan are also eligible for a grant or short-term loan from the 'Access to Learning Fund'. This is administered by the university on a case-by-case basis. As well as these facilities, universities will have a hardship fund for students in difficult situations, while banks also offer loans of up to £20000 at higher rates of interest.

The counterweight to these potential debts has been the comparatively high level of job security in medicine, although, with increased competition as discussed above, job security for life is in no way guaranteed. However, for many students, despite the academic demands of the course, a part-time job is essential to help cover costs and maintain a comfortable standard of living, with some students working up to 20 hours a week.

Working abroad

www.bma.org.uk/careers/working_abroad/Workingabroadguide.jsp

Being a doctor has long been considered a passport to the wider world. Indeed, although plans to do so must be well thought out and there may be a lot of preparation to achieve this, there is a lot to be gained from working abroad.

Some people choose to leave temporarily, whereas others move for good. Those who leave in the middle of training need to be particularly careful that they have permission to do so from their deanery so that they will be able to resume training seamlessly on return. In some circumstances, training overseas can be integrated into UK postgraduate training.

Health-care systems vary in their set-up and quality from country to country. Some people choose to go to developing countries where resources are sparse, whereas others go to other developed countries. Regardless, it is important to bear in mind the impact of any language barriers.

The developing world

The 2007 government report by Lord Nigel Crisp, the former Chief Executive of the NHS, on 'Global Health Partnerships' (known as the 'Crisp Report') has identified the role that British health-care professionals can play in developing countries. It encouraged doctors and other professionals to take time out to work in these countries, although concrete mechanisms to facilitate this process within the NHS have yet to be established.

Working in a developing country is a demanding, yet satisfying, challenge. Doctors in these settings are often under little supervision and need to be confident in what they are doing. As well as being able to provide clinical services, they also need to be able to train local health workers in order to improve the long-term medical infrastructure.

There are many non-governmental organizations (NGOs) that work in developing countries. These include the Red Cross/Red Crescent, Médecins Sans Frontières (MSF) and Medical Emergency Relief International (MERLIN). NGOs also send doctors into war zones to treat casualties of conflict, as well as into refugee camps.

Most organizations expect doctors to have obtained at least 2 years of postgraduate training, and consultants are especially valued. They usually provide for subsistence, flights and insurance as well as a modest salary. Placements can last from 9 months to 3 years.

European Economic Area and Switzerland

The main obstacle to moving to another country in the European Economic Area (EEA) is the language barrier. Otherwise, moving is easy, because there is no need to take any exams or obtain a work permit.

The other countries in the EEA at present are: Austria, Belgium, Bulgaria, Cyprus, Czech Republic, Denmark, Estonia, Finland, France, Germany, Greece, Hungary, Iceland, Ireland, Italy, Liechtenstein, Latvia, Lithuania, Luxembourg, Netherlands, Malta, Norway, Poland, Portugal, Romania, Slovakia, Slovenia, Spain and Sweden.

Australia, New Zealand and Canada

These countries receive many British graduates both temporarily and permanently. Doctors are able to work in largely public health-care systems and to practise in English, while also having the opportunity to experience medicine in remote areas. Specialty training programmes are also relatively similar to those in the UK.

In Australia and New Zealand, there are rules restricting overseas doctors from practising in positions that could be filled by a local doctor. To practise in Canada, doctors need to have passed examinations set by the Medical Council of Canada, which test competency, knowledge, skills and attitudes.

The USA

Although for most destinations it is acceptable to make any plans to leave the UK after graduation, the earlier that you decide on whether or not you intend to move to the USA the better, even as a medical student.

To obtain a postgraduate training position (known as a 'residency'), you need to pass the US Medical Licensing Examination (USMLE) Steps 1 and 2. These are national exams taken by all American medical students. The exams are expensive (especially Step 2) and you must be committed to doing extra work for them.

Step 1 covers basic medical science, which is covered by most UK medical schools in the first 2 years. The optimal time to take this exam is therefore at the end of Year 2. However, the syllabus is not like for like and you need to invest in books and possibly special revision courses in order to score highly. The format of the exam also requires some getting used to as it is 7 hours of 336 computer-based multiple choice questions. This can be taken at exam centres in the UK. Many residency programmes use the score from Step 1 as the barometer for eligibility.

Step 2 is made up of a clinical knowledge (CK) exam, which is similar in format to Step 1, and a clinical skills (CS) exam, which must be taken in one of five US exam centres. It is best taken after Year 4 or 5 in the UK. Step 3 is an examination of diagnostic and patient management skills. It is taken at the end of the first year of residency.

The American health-care system is very different to the UK and many other countries. As it is a privatized system where most people have to pay for insurance, it has often come under strong criticism as being unacceptable in the developed world for widening inequalities.

Junior doctors in the USA work much longer hours than in the UK or the EU. However, this results in a shorter length of training after which you can work as an attending specialist (equivalent to consultant) and you may progress to professorships. Diagnostic and therapeutic options available for doctors are among the most technologically advanced and, at a senior level, doctors can potentially make considerable sums of money. On the downside, there is the serious challenge of endemic litigation.

Hours and pay

Similar to training, there have been significant changes made to working patterns of doctors. Due to the European Working Time Directive (EWTD), workers should not work more than 48 hours a week and have requirements on the amount of rest that they should have. The NHS has set the target for implementing this by August 2009.

This is far removed from the recent past where doctors sometimes worked over 100 hours a week. Nowadays, doctors are usually employed on a partial shift basis. This means that they normally work 9am to 5pm and have a rota for night and weekend shifts. When they do these shifts, they usually have the following day off to rest. A&E doctors have a full shift rota.

When it comes to working hours, theory can be very different to practice. Many junior doctors are expected to arrive at 7am and, if the workload has not been completed, they can often work until 7pm. It is also difficult to monitor the rest requirements of the EWTD and they may not always be enforced by all hospitals.

Although it is true that junior doctors were overworked and many were burnt out, there are fears that the reduction in hours will result in an inexperienced work force. Some are also concerned that there is inadequate continuity of care, because patients see different doctors every day. Others argue that the quality of experiences gained with extra rest will be greater, as well as the safety aspect for patients.

Most doctors will earn enough to live a comfortable lifestyle, although there are few who become super-rich. Given the potential earnings in other sectors, it would be unwise to choose a career in medicine purely for the money. An important consideration to bear in mind when thinking about money is that medicine can also be a 5- or 6-year degree with fees (up to £3175) and a student loan (up to £4600 outside London and up to £6475 in London) that has to be paid back after graduation. An NHS bursary is provided after Year 4 to help, but the burden can still be a heavy one to bear. The big advantage of a medical career is that very few doctors are unemployed (currently) and the job security is superior to that in most other sectors (currently!).

Junior doctors' pay is banded according to the job in which they work. Banding supplements a proportion of the basic salary depending on how many hours a week the doctor works and how intense the work is:

1C = less than 48 hours per week working on call from home = 20%

1B = less than 48 hours per week at a low intensity at less unsocial times = 40%

1A = less than 48 hours per week at a high intensity and at unsocial times = 50%

2B = between 48 and 56 hours per week at a low intensity at less unsocial times = 50%

2A = between 48 and 56 hours per week at a high intensity and at unsocial times = 80%

3 = over 56 hours per week = 100%.

However, in practice, this too is poorly enforced because trusts tend not to measure how hard and when each doctor is working, and banding is often arbitrary. In addition to banding, those working in London will receive weighting of up to £2162 per year, depending on where their place of work is. From August 2009, bands 2 and 3 should no longer exist.

The minimum junior doctor salaries before tax are as follows (based on band 1C):

FY1 = £26 200
FY2 = £32 500
SHO = £32 500
Registrar = £36 300.

Many doctors find themselves earning slightly more than this, but band 3 jobs are rare! Currently, most jobs are in 1A or 2B, resulting in a 50% supplement to basic pay. In addition to these salaries, doctors can also work locum shifts, which are paid on an hourly basis. Depending on the hours and the type of shift being worked and for how long, there can be a healthy bonus, with hourly rates ranging from £20 for FY2 doctors to £25 for registrars. Locum jobs can be done at the doctor's employing trust or through an agency at a different trust.

Hospital consultant pay is much more complicated and potential earnings vary for different specialties. NHS pay is based on the out-of-hours intensity of the work and seniority. A study published in 2008 in the *Journal of the Royal Society of Medicine* found that the mean NHS income for consultants in most hospital specialties was between £70 000 and £80 000 a year. Cardiothoracic surgeons earn the most, with a mean of £95 000. When private income is also taken into account, around half of the specialties earned in excess of £100 000 a year, with plastic surgery at the top of the pile, with just under £220 000 a year. It is important to note that private practice can be very competitive (especially in the big cities), annual income is not guaranteed (and therefore cannot be relied upon for day-to-day living) and it essentially involves running a separate business in addition to your NHS practice, which can take up a significant portion of your free time and upset your work–life balance.

As a result of the GMS contract, there is no recommended salary for general practice partners. They should study the accounts of the practice and determine how much of the profits they will be sharing. Salaried GPs earn at least £52 500, although there is no limit on how much practices will offer to pay them. General practice partners can earn considerably more but have the added hassle of running their practice business.

Other career options

If for one reason or another you are not entirely satisfied with medicine, you should at least consider some of the other options. There are many different areas that bright students can go into such as:

- academia – working at a university conducting research
- accountancy
- actuary – mathematicians who study the financial impact of risks to businesses
- architecture
- biotechnology

- business
- computing
- corporate finance
- dentistry
- engineering
- investment banking
- journalism
- law
- optics/optometry
- pharmacy
- psychology
- teaching
- veterinary medicine.

3 Getting the grades

So you're caught up in the excitement of becoming a doctor. You've done all the right things – you ace the UKCAT, the application referees are blown away by your commitment, the interviewers think that you're God's gift to the medical school, that place is yours – almost! There is one condition that you MUST satisfy to get in: the grades.

No matter how often you hear that A levels are being dumbed down, they are still a formidable challenge that requires hard work and the right mentality. It is vital that you make the right choices to ensure that you don't stumble at this important hurdle.

How A levels work

A levels currently take the form of a modular 2-year course, with each subject consisting of four or six units. In the first year, you complete two or three units in at least four subjects to make up your AS levels. In the second year, you complete the remaining two or three units (known as A2), which upgrade your AS results into complete A-level grades. Most students are advised to discontinue one of the four subjects at this stage so that they can focus on the more rigorous units of A2.

Each unit may be examined by written papers, oral tests for languages, coursework or a combination of these. Exams can be sat either in January or in May/June, and you are allowed to repeat units in order to maximize your score.

You should also remember that the scores that you obtain as you go along are in many ways more important than the grades to which they equate. The standardized scoring system that is used is called the Uniform Mark Scale (UMS). AS and A2 each have a maximum of 300 UMS points. An A grade is equivalent to 80% (240 at AS, 480 in a full A level), and a B grade is 70%. The grades themselves become of relevance only when you submit your AS grades on your UCAS form and when you receive your overall results at the very end.

Relating your A-level choices to medicine can make interviews smoother and can make you better motivated.

Choosing the right subjects

All of the medical schools have their own entry requirements and, at the very least, these stipulate that applicants have completed AS levels in biology and/or chemistry. To maximize your coverage of medical schools, it is advisable to choose both of these subjects.

If there are any medical schools to which you are particularly keen to apply, you should ensure that your A-level choices meet their requirements. This is especially true for some Oxbridge colleges, which expect a strong grounding in science.

There are a number of factors that you need to consider when choosing the remaining two subjects:

- **Availability:** make sure that the subjects are offered by your school or college and that they fit into your timetable.
- **Confidence:** you must know that you have the potential to get A grades in these subjects.
- **Interest:** you need be motivated by the content of these courses.
- **Usefulness:** think about what demonstrable skills and knowledge you will gain from these courses.

The last point is pertinent but often missed by a number of students. If you are able to evaluate how your A-level choices can be put into a medical context and how they are going to make you a more rounded and interesting medical student, you need to be able to impress this on the medical schools to which you've applied.

Below are the benefits that we think you could gain from a number of the subjects on offer and are worth considering:

Sciences

Physics

Taking physics will make you a well-rounded scientist. The exams also carry themselves in the same vein as biology and chemistry, so adjusting between the subjects shouldn't be too difficult.

The exam boards offer an optional unit in medical physics and, if possible, this can help you familiarize yourself with the role of physics in medical specialties such as radiology and anaesthesia.

Maths

The benefits of maths are probably more abstract than concrete, but the subject does equip you with the fundamental skills of logical reasoning that every good scientist needs. If you choose the right units, you will also be introduced to basic statistics, which underpins medical research. If you prefer dealing with equations rather than sentences, there's little reason not to go for it.

Psychology

Psychology is specifically relevant to neurology and psychiatry, as it provides an understanding of how mental processes develop from both biological and social perspectives. It also provides an introduction to research methods and case studies involving humans.

When medical schools refer to 'sciences' in their subject entry requirements, this does not include psychology.

Humanities and social sciences

Geography

This is broadly divided into human and physical geography. Human geography centres on issues such as food supply, population dynamics and public health, both locally and internationally. The fieldwork might also offer opportunities to carry out investigations on public health.

Business studies

While traditionally this is not a subject that would be promoted, there are many quarters of the medical profession that are encouraging students and doctors to gain knowledge and skills in business and management, and some medical schools are even driving it into their curriculum.

You can put what you learn in the context of NHS trusts and individual GP practices. If possible, you could carry out your coursework project on a GP practice and also spend time with the practice manager to appreciate how it is run under the General Medical Services (GMS) contract.

Economics

Economics is studied from a wider scientific perspective and is probably as useful as anything in providing you with an understanding of society as a whole. You can apply your knowledge to understand government health policy, not just in Britain, but globally.

Philosophy

The study of philosophy provides grounding in critical thinking and rational argument, skills that can be applied to any field.

Doctors need to be specifically aware of ethical medical practice and you will certainly be advantaged for Section 3 of the BMAT, which may be used in your interview.

Modern foreign languages

At A level, as well as enhancing your proficiency in communication, you will also be expected to have a deeper understanding of the countries that speak the language. Take this opportunity to study the standard of health and the health-care systems of these countries. If possible, do your oral presentation or written coursework on this aspect.

Your school may also offer the opportunity to visit the country as part of an exchange programme. See if you can arrange a day or so of work experience in a hospital or with a community doctor, after which, you can compare and contrast it with your experiences in the NHS. This is likely to require a lot of planning and negotiation, but it is possible and is definitely worthwhile!

Others

Subjects such as *classical languages* and *English language* and/or *literature* are also well respected and academically rooted. If you have a specific interest or strength in these, then they should also be considered.

How to approach A levels

There are two points that you need to take on board to be successful at A level.

Set yourself high standards

Keep pushing your boundaries and always look for areas to improve, even if they're small. Scraping an A at AS level may be satisfying, but bear in mind that you will have little margin for error at A2.

You should also remember that UMS points do not necessarily reflect your performance on paper. The scores are standardized by the exam boards, so, if many students do well, the marks will be readjusted accordingly.

Setting yourself high standards is also the best way to impress your teachers, because they value hard work above anything else and respond by giving you a glowing reference on your UCAS form, with optimistic predicted grades.

Practice makes perfect – the exam boards have past papers and you should get your hands on as many as possible. Keep having a go at these and learn from any mistakes. The style and content of questions remain fairly similar within each exam board, so it is a good way to familiarize yourself and be prepared.

Be organized and strategic – take control!

Make the most of the exam schedule – if your school or college doesn't offer January sittings, there are a number of approved centres that do at a small cost and, as long as you notify the exam board, your scores can be validated and put towards your final grade. If you are going down this route, make arrangements early to save costs.

Get planning early – as soon as you start your AS levels, work out how many exams you will have over the 2 years and plan realistically when you're going to sit each one. You should think about a 'plan B' in case things don't pan out so smoothly.

If you choose to take exams in January, make the most of them – use them to motivate you to work hard in the autumn term and bear in mind that, if you score highly enough, it'll be a big weight off your shoulders in the summer.

If you get a fairly good result but feel that there's scope for improvement, you might want to consider retaking that exam, because every mark that you gain in a unit that you're good at is a mark that you can afford to lose in one that you find harder going.

To illustrate these points, let's take an example of how one medical student went about taking A-level maths.

Year 1 January: Core 1 (78/100 UMS)

Year 1 May: Core 1 repeat (99/100)

                                    Mechanics 1 (85/100)

                                    Statistics 1 (76/100)

UMS so far: 99 + 86 + 76 = 261/300

AS grade: A (≥240)

Year 2 January: Mechanics 1 repeat (95/100)

                                    Statistics 1 repeat (84/100)

                                    Core 2 (77/100)

                                    Statistics 2 (94/100)

UMS so far: 99 + 95 + 84 + 77 + 94 = 449/500

Year 2 June: Core 3 (41/100)
Total UMS: 449 + 41 = 490/600

A-level grade: A (≥480)

Despite scoring a meagre 41% (equivalent to E grade!) in his final unit, he received an overall A grade because he accumulated high UMS points in the easier units. By identifying his strengths in maths, he was able to focus his attention on the more challenging biology and chemistry exams at the end.

Arrange to sit exams in January and May/June so that you have a manageable workload at all times and are able to optimize your scores.

Doing well at biology and chemistry

Biology and chemistry can be very difficult. Students can find that there is a big jump between GCSE and AS level, especially for those who took Double Award Science. If you can anticipate this jump and get into the swing of things early, it will pay off as you get closer to the exams.

The worst thing that you can do is to fall into the trap of denial and overconfidence. This is something that mostly concerns students who did well at GCSEs without too much effort. A-level science is a completely different ballgame, with some challenging concepts with which you need to get to grips. All it takes is a couple of tricky questions to throw you off track.

 Do NOT be overconfident about biology and chemistry – they are much harder than they were at GCSE!

Here are a few tips that will hopefully make life easier:

- If you are struggling, get help early – don't hang around. Most teachers like being asked for help and will take their time to guide you. Some of your fellow students might also have ways to help you understand. This is a good way to keep each other motivated and foster a healthy classroom environment.
- Get yourself a good revision guide – look for the books that are endorsed by your exam board and, if they are both thorough and accessible in style, they are the ones to go for. If this isn't good enough, go for an unofficial guide for your particular specification.
- Understanding beats memorizing – a powerful memory can help, but knowing how everything works will mean that you can tackle any problem in the exam.

- Get your hands on the right past papers and mark schemes – use the papers from your board but stick to the modern ones. These are the most accurate way of keeping an eye on your progress. If there are particular questions that you are stuck with and can't figure out despite the mark schemes, get your teacher to clear it up for you.
- Planning: be prepared for coursework and essays. Make sure that you're well aware of what is expected of you and don't give away any easy marks. If your synopsis paper involves an essay, make sure that you practise a few titles and get into the habit of bringing in different aspects of the course and putting them together.
- Courses: there are some very helpful revision courses available that usually take place in the Easter holidays before the exam period. These can be quite costly, and it is important that you get feedback from students who have attended them before so that you don't end up wasting your time or money.

Results day

All A-level results come out on the third Thursday in August – make sure that you're in the country for this and that you're able to go to your school or college bright and early to pick them up. Leaving it until it arrives in the post the next day could make all the difference – and this goes for those with and those without offers.

You may be very confident, but preparing for the worst is never a bad thing. Take the phone numbers of the medical schools to which you've applied with you. Also have a look for other less competitive courses that you wouldn't mind undertaking if you couldn't get into medicine. If you've narrowly missed out (e.g. AAC for an ABB offer), call up the medical school that offered you a place and plead your case with them. They may be able to accommodate you or defer your entry.

You should also prepare for 'clearing'. This is the process where any unfulfilled vacancies are free to apply for. The clearing places will be advertised in the broadsheet newspapers, so make sure that you have a copy. If you haven't received an offer but have the required grades, there may be a few places available in medicine for which you can apply.

Be aware that medical schools sometimes send misleading letters before A-level results arrive. They receive your results a few days before you do, and may send you a letter of congratulations or an apology. They have been known to get these letters wrong in the past, so do go in and check on the day.

4 Choosing the right medical school

Medicine is unusual in that, regardless of where you graduate, the degree is worth exactly the same. Despite this, medical schools vary greatly. Different students have different expectations and you need to determine what your priorities are when making your choice. Even though there are five spaces on the UCAS form, only four applications for medicine are allowed. Each choice that you make is a precious one, and you need to take your time and consider your options. You should be reassured that medical schools cannot tell where else you have applied unless you have also chosen another course at the same university.

In this chapter, we discuss some of the factors that you need to consider when making your choice.

Entry requirements

First and foremost, be aware of the entry requirements of each medical school and make sure that you fulfil the criteria for any to which you apply. By and large, those students who don't are discarded immediately from the admissions process.

The requirements are very strict and they vary between medical schools. They also change year on year, so it is important to be certain before you submit your UCAS form. It's a good idea to pick at least one medical school with lower final grade requirements as an insurance policy.

Up-to-date entry requirements can be found on the medical school websites. The School of Medicine at Cardiff University compiles the UKMedSchool Guide each year, which is an excellent survey of the requirements of all medical schools. It can be found online at: www.cardiff.ac.uk/medic/degreeprogrammes/resources/UKM edSchool%20Guide%202008%20b.pdf.

Short-listing policies

It is a good idea for you to get in touch with the medical schools to which you have applied and confirm their policies for interview short listing. At some medical schools, predicted grades lower than the entry requirements and low marks in the admissions tests can result in rejection, even before the personal statement is read! For example, it may be pointless applying to one of these schools if you have a low UKCAT score. At others, all of these components are scored individually and an overall mark dictates who will get an interview.

Curricular differences

Course structures and teaching methods vary greatly between medical schools and some may suit your needs better than others.

Course structure

Traditional courses

In the pre-clinical years, the traditional courses teach the basic medical sciences as individual subjects. This means that subjects such as anatomy, physiology, pathology and pharmacology are taught separately and in great depth. Traditionalists believe that students must have a good grounding in these areas as a solid foundation on which clinical practice can be built. The universities that retain this structure are Oxford, Cambridge and St Andrew's (Bute Medical School), although the last incorporates a reasonable amount of early patient contact. These universities all run 6-year courses, including a research project in Year 3, which culminate in a BA (Bachelor of Arts) or BSc (Bachelor of Science).

Integrated courses

Modern courses integrate the basic sciences for each body system, e.g. the cardiovascular system or the musculoskeletal system. Often, this also involves some exposure to patients and learning basic clinical skills. Advocates of this structure believe that it brings the basic sciences to life and puts them in a more accessible context for students.

Teaching methods

Different teaching methods are employed to varying extents by the medical schools. This mainly applies to the pre-clinical phase of training. Attending taster courses at different schools or even arranging to observe teaching sessions may allow you to appreciate what suits you. It is also a good idea to ask any medical schools in which you are interested for a typical first-year weekly timetable to get an accurate impression of the weekly academic commitments of a medical student. Although some methods may seem more appealing to you than others at this stage, you should also weigh this against your adaptability when considering all the other factors.

Lectures

Lectures are the traditional teaching method and remain the most widely used. They involve a teacher speaking to many students in a large lecture theatre. This didactic method means that the teacher has control over what the students are supposed to learn and keeps them on the right track. However, because of the large size of the groups, there is little opportunity for interaction, and hours of lectures can be uninspiring.

Tutorials

In tutorials, there is greater scope for interaction between teachers and students, which means that students are actively involved in the learning process. Teachers are also able to directly test the student's knowledge. However, as many teachers are required, some may not be as good as others. Not all medical schools employ tutorials.

Problem-based learning

www.bmj.com/cgi/reprint/326/7384/328.pdf

Problem-based learning (PBL) is another small-group learning method, where the teacher 'facilitates' the session as opposed to actively teaching. Students are given a scenario from which they brainstorm learning objectives. They then go away and research the objectives independently before reconvening after a few days to discuss their findings. This allows students to direct their learning and improve their team working skills. On the downside, there may be less standardization of what students learn and there may be discrepancies in the quality of facilitators. Some medical schools do not use PBL at all, whereas for others it is the main feature of the curriculum.

Dissection

Anatomical teaching methods are a highly contentious issue. Dissection continues to be used by many medical schools, usually with a small group of students dissecting a cadaver on a weekly basis under the supervision of a demonstrator. However, because of limited resources and question marks over its value, other medical schools use alternative techniques to teach anatomy, including the use of prosected cadavers, which have already been dissected to show important structures. There is also increasing use of computer-assisted learning with the emergence of highly detailed, three-dimensional, anatomical representations.

Intercalated degrees

http://archive.student.bmj.com/back_issues/1101/careers/418.html

Approximately one-third of all medical students undertake an intercalated degree. This is an additional bachelor's degree in a specific subject, usually taken over an extra year. It is an advisable option for students with ambitions of working in academic medicine, although it comes at the cost of a year where you could be earning. Most intercalated degrees involve a research project that may open doors to presentations and publications, as well as the educational experiences of lab work or clinical data collection and critical appraisal of medical literature.

At most medical schools, the intercalated degree is optional and students can compete for what is available. However, at a few others, it is compulsory for all undergraduate students:

- Cambridge
- Imperial
- Nottingham (no additional year of study – part of the 5-year programme)
- Oxford
- St Andrew's
- UCL.

Nottingham awards an intercalated BMedSci (Bachelor of Medical Science) to all medical students as part of the standard 5-year programme. Although this is technically of the same value as all other bachelor's degrees, it is worth less than an intercalated degree from the other medical schools on the current Foundation Programme application. That being said, there are similar educational benefits and opportunities for presentation and publication.

Some schools give you the opportunity to choose from a wide range of subjects, even extending into non-medical realms, whereas others are limited to basic medical sciences. It is sometimes possible to transfer to a different medical school to undertake an intercalated degree, although this may involve extensive competition.

Cambridge, Leicester and UCL also offer MB PhD programmes to a few well-performing students, and these are often also open to external students. This extends the medical course to 8 years but can set a future academic doctor well on his or her way.

If you do not find an intercalated degree relevant or appealing at this stage, you should think twice about applying to the schools where it is compulsory. Otherwise, this is unlikely to be a crucial factor on which to base your decision. If you have any particular interests, have a look on www.intercalate.co.uk to see where these are catered for.

Location

Going to medical school often means moving from home, and, considering that you will be based at a particular medical school for up to 6 years, it is important to be happy with your surroundings. Nothing beats visiting the medical schools in which you are interested before applying and taking a good look around.

Many medical schools are based in large cities, whereas others are in smaller towns. Some are part of large campuses where all the facilities from the halls of residence to the libraries, classrooms and lecture theatres are in the same place, whereas others are scattered around smaller campuses or in the buildings surrounding a teaching hospital.

Living costs also vary from city to city, including in halls of residence. London in particular is notoriously expensive, whereas places such as Leeds, Sheffield and Durham have cheaper expenses and rents.

The social life at the university and in the surrounding area is also important. The local medical students can be helpful in telling you where the best places to hang out are, as well as any particular advantages and disadvantages to the area.

You might also think about what you are going to see and experience in the local teaching hospitals. In certain areas you will receive a broader exposure to diseases because of richer cultural diversity and health inequalities. Some hospitals may also be specialist centres of excellence in a particular field of interest.

Oxbridge

The Universities of Oxford and Cambridge are different to the other UK medical schools due to their collegiate system. Colleges have a lot of autonomy over the application process and are able to dictate their own selection policies to a certain extent. If you choose to apply to one of these universities, it is important to bear that in mind and ensure that you choose a college for which you are eligible. During the pre-clinical phase, the colleges play an important role by providing regular academic tutorials for each student, alongside the lectures and practicals provided by the university medical faculty.

At the end of the pre-clinical phase (Year 3), students are awarded a BA. Interestingly, this can be upgraded to an MA (Master of Arts) for a fee soon after qualifying as a doctor. For clinical studies, approximately half the students will transfer either between the two universities or to one of the schools in London.

Visit the medical schools!

The best way to maximize your insight into the different medical schools is to visit them and speak to students and staff. This can be through an open day, or you could arrange a visit alone or with friends by contacting the admissions team. If this is during term time, you might be able to catch a peek of what different classes are like. If you are thinking about living in university accommodation, it is important that you have a look around the halls of residences as well as the surrounding area.

Some medical schools offer taster courses and these can give you an appreciation of the facilities available as well as how the style of teaching works. By contacting the admissions team early, you can make sure that you secure yourself a place!

The medical schools

www.medschoolsonline.co.uk

Below is a list of all the UK medical schools, with the relevant web and email addresses. A lot of information is available online, but, if you cannot find what you are looking for, get in touch with the schools and find out what you need to know. It can be particularly useful to find out the recent admissions statistics and the short-listing policies so you can make a fully informed and strategic choice.

Degree titles

- MB, BM = Bachelor of Medicine
- BS, ChB, BCh, BChir = Bachelor of Surgery
- BAO = Bachelor in the Art of Obstetrics.

The medical degrees awarded by the different schools result in various combinations of the above abbreviations. However, they all amount to the equivalent of one medical degree; i.e. although the University of Southampton only awards BM, whereas Queen's University Belfast awards MB BCh BAO, there is no difference in value, and the Belfast graduate is no more qualified in surgery or obstetrics and holds no advantage in postgraduate training in these fields.

Aberdeen

5-year MB BCh (A100)
www.abdn.ac.uk/medicine-dentistry/medical-dental/prospective

Key contact

Dr Kath Greaves – k.greaves@abdn.ac.uk
Associate Dean for Admissions

Barts and The London

5-year MB BS (A100)
www.smd.qmul.ac.uk/undergraduate/mbbs

4-year MB BS Graduate Entry Programme (A101)
www.smd.qmul.ac.uk/undergraduate/graduateentry

Key contacts

Dr Cathy Baker – c.s.baker@qmul.ac.uk
Admissions Tutor
Christine Sofianos – c.m.sofianos@qmul.ac.uk
Admissions Manager

Birmingham

5-year MB ChB (A100)
www.medicine.bham.ac.uk/ug/mbchb

4-year MB BCh Graduate Entry (A101)
www.medicine.bham.ac.uk/ug/gec

Key contact

Professor Chris Lote – c.j.lote@bham.ac.uk
Admissions Tutor

Brighton and Sussex

5-year BM BS (A100)
www.bsms.ac.uk/undergraduate/5-year

Key contact

Professor John Kay – j.e.kay@bsms.ac.uk
Admissions Tutor

Bristol

5-year MB ChB (A100)
www.medici.bris.ac.uk/general/Undergraduate

4-year MB ChB Fast-Track Graduate Entry (A101)
www.medici.bris.ac.uk/general/Undergraduate/graduate.html

6-year MB ChB Premedical (A104)
www.medici.bris.ac.uk/general/Undergraduate/premed.html

Key contacts

Matt Holt – Matthew.Holt@bristol.ac.uk
Admissions Co-ordinator
med-admissions@bristol.ac.uk
Medical Admissions Office

Cambridge

6-year MB BChir + BA (A100)
www.cam.ac.uk/admissions/undergraduate/courses/medicine

Colleges
Available at all colleges except Homerton and Hughes Hall

4-year MB BChir Graduate Course (A101)
www.cam.ac.uk/admissions/undergraduate/courses/medgrad

Colleges
Hughes Hall
Lucy Cavendish (women only)
Wolfson

Key contacts

www.cam.ac.uk/admissions/undergraduate/colleges

Please contact the admissions tutors for each college directly as policies and practices can vary.

Cardiff

5-year MB ChB (A100)
www.cardiff.ac.uk/medic/degreeprogrammes/undergraduate/
fiveyearmedicineprogramme

6-year MB ChB Foundation (A104)
www.cardiff.ac.uk/medic/degreeprogrammes/undergraduate/
undergraduateadmissions/foundation

Key contacts

Professor Geraint Williams – WilliamsGT@cf.ac.uk
Sub-Dean for Medical Admissions
Shona McGlynn – medicaladmissions@cardiff.ac.uk
Admissions Office

Dundee

5-year MB ChB (A100)
www.dundee.ac.uk/undergraduate/courses/medicine.htm

6-year MB ChB Pre-medical (A104)
www.dundee.ac.uk/undergraduate/courses/medicine.htm

Key contact

Gordon Black – g.g.black@dundee.ac.uk
Admissions Officer

East Anglia

5-year MB BS (A100)
www.uea.ac.uk/med/course/mbbs?mode=cm

6-year MB BS Foundation (A104)
www.uea.ac.uk/med/course/6mbms?mode=cm

Key contact

Natasha Gales – Med.admiss@uea.ac.uk
Senior Admissions Assistant

Edinburgh

5-year MB ChB (A100)
www.ed.ac.uk/schools-departments/medicine-vet-medicine/
undergraduate/medicine

Key contacts

Dr Donald Thomson – Donald.Thomson@ed.ac.uk
Director of Admissions
Ginny Allan – medug@ed.ac.uk
Admissions Officer

Glasgow

5-year MB ChB (A100)
www.gla.ac.uk/faculties/medicine/undergraduatestudy/medicine/
mbchbdegreeprogramme/admissions

Key contact

Colleen Doherty – admissions@clinmed.gla.ac.uk
Admissions Administrator

Hull–York

5-year MB BS (A100)
www.hyms.ac.uk/admissions

Key contacts

Dr Jane Adam – jane.adam@hyms.ac.uk
Associate Dean for Admissions
Jane Pearce – jane.pearce@hyms.ac.uk
Admissions Officer

Imperial

6-year MB BS + BSc (A100)
www1.imperial.ac.uk/medicine/teaching/undergraduate/medicine/
admissions

4-year MB BS Graduate Entry (A101)
www1.imperial.ac.uk/medicine/teaching/undergraduate/ge/admission

Key contact

Professor John Laycock – j.laycock@imperial.ac.uk
Admissions Tutor

Keele

5-year MB ChB (A100)
www.keele.ac.uk/depts/ms/undergrad

4-year MB ChB Fast-track (A101)
www.keele.ac.uk/depts/ms/undergrad/courseinfo/entryrequirements.
htm

6-year MB ChB Health Foundation (A104)
www.keele.ac.uk/depts/ms/undergrad/courseinfo/entryrequirements.
htm

Key contacts

Dr Gordon Dent – g.dent@hfac.keele.ac.uk
Director of Admissions
Julia Molyneux – j.m.molyneux@hfac.keele.ac.uk
Admissions Manager

King's (Guy's, King's and St Thomas'/GKT)

5-year MB BS (A100)
www.kcl.ac.uk/ugp10/programme/85

4-year MB BS Graduate/Professional Entry Programme (A102)
www.kcl.ac.uk/ugp10/programme/649

6-year MB BS Extended Medical Degree Programme (A101)
www.kcl.ac.uk/ugp10/programme/687

Key contacts

Dr Graham Clayden – graham.clayden@kcl.ac.uk
Sub Dean Student Admissions

Leeds

5-year MB ChB (A100)
www.leeds.ac.uk/medicine/admissions

Key contacts

Dr Caroline Wilson – ugmadmissions@leeds.ac.uk
Sub Dean for Admissions
Ann Gaunt – a.e.gaunt@leeds.ac.uk
Admissions Co-ordinator

Leicester

5-year MB ChB (A100)
www.le.ac.uk/sm/le/a100

4-year MB ChB Graduate Entry (A101)
www.le.ac.uk/sm/le/A101_Health Sciences

Key contacts

Dr Kevin West – med-admis@leicester.ac.uk
Senior Tutor for Admissions
Dr Laura Mongan – med-admis@leicester.ac.uk
Graduate Admission Tutor

Lincoln

1-year Certificate in Health Science (Medicine) (B790)
www.lincoln.ac.uk/fabs/_courses/undergraduate/health_science/
default.asp

On completion of this Certificate, students transfer to the
University of Nottingham for the 5-year BM BS + BMedSci
course

Key contact

Emma Jubbs – ejubbs@lincoln.ac.uk
Marketing and Recruitment Officer

Liverpool

5-year MB ChB (A100)
www.liv.ac.uk/sme/prospective/entry_mbchb.htm

5-year MB ChB based at Lancaster University (A105)
www.liv.ac.uk/sme/prospective/lancaster.htm

4-year MB ChB (A101)
www.liv.ac.uk/sme/prospective/graduate.htm

Key contacts

Dr Fiona Watson – F.Watson01@liverpool.ac.uk
Director of Admissions
Joanna Henderson – Joanneh@liverpool.ac.uk
Admissions Officer

Manchester

5-year MB ChB (A106)
www.manchester.ac.uk/undergraduate/courses/search/atoz/course/
?code=01428

6-year MB ChB Foundation (A104)
www.manchester.ac.uk/undergraduate/courses/search/atoz/course/
?code=01430

Key contacts

Professor David Yates – david.yates@manchester.ac.uk
Director of Admissions
Ms Linda Harding – linda.m.harding@manchester.ac.uk
Admissions Manager

Newcastle/Durham

5-year MB BS (A100)
www.ncl.ac.uk/undergraduate/course/A100/Medicine_and_Surgery

4-year MB BS (Accelerated Programme) (A101)
www.ncl.ac.uk/undergraduate/course/A101/Medicine_and_Surgery_
(Accelerated_Programme)

Key contacts

Dianorah Smith – dianorah.smith@ncl.ac.uk
Admissions Administrator

Nottingham

5-year MB BS + BMedSci (A100)
www.nottingham.ac.uk/ugstudy/course.php?code=000001

4-year MB BS (A101)
www.nottingham.ac.uk/ugstudy/course.php?code=012760

Key contacts

Martine Lowes – martine.lowes@nottingham.ac.uk
A100 Admissions Officer
Cathy Porter – cathy.porter@nottingham.ac.uk
A101 Admissions Officer

Oxford

6-year BM BCh + BA (A100)
www.medsci.ox.ac.uk/study/medicine

Colleges

Available at all colleges except Harris Manchester and Mansfield.

4-year BM BCh Accelerated (A101)
http://bmra.pharm.ox.ac.uk

Colleges

Eleven colleges offer this course.

Key contacts

Admissions Office – admissions@medschool.ox.ac.uk
Dr Paul Dennis – paul.dennis@pharm.ox.ac.uk
Academic Head of Accelerated Course
Lesley Maitland – lesley.maitland@medsci.ox.ac.uk
Accelerated Course Administrator

Peninsula

5-year BM BS (A100)
www.pcmd.ac.uk/pms/undergraduate/index.php

Key contacts

Dr David Bristow – david.bristow@pms.ac.uk
Director of Undergraduate Medical Studies
Sue Locke – sue.locke@pms.ac.uk
Senior Undergraduate Admissions Coordinator

Queen's University Belfast

5-year MB BCh BAO (A100)
www.qub.ac.uk/home/ProspectiveStudents/FindaCourse/ucf/
CourseInformation/index.html?id=A1

Key contacts

Jennifer Dwyer – admissions@qub.ac.uk
Head of Admissions

Sheffield

5-year MB ChB (A100)
www.shef.ac.uk/medicine/prospective_ug/mbchb

6-year MB ChB Pre-medical (A104)
www.shef.ac.uk/prospectus/courseDetails.do?id=3620182009

Key contacts

Dr Martin Lennard – M.S.Lennard@sheffield.ac.uk
Undergraduate Dean for Admissions
Siobhan Marples – medadmissions@sheffield.ac.uk
Medical Admissions Officer

Southampton

5-year BM (A100)
www.som.soton.ac.uk/undergrad/course/bm5

4-year BM Graduate Entry (A101)
www.som.soton.ac.uk/undergrad/course/bm4

6-year BM Widening Access (A102)
www.som.soton.ac.uk/undergrad/course/bm6

Key contacts

Dr Chris Stephens – crs1@southampton.ac.uk
Director of Education
Amanda Spencer – Bmadmissions@soton.ac.uk
Admissions Manager

St Andrew's (Bute)

6-year BSc + MB ChB (A100)
http://medicine.st-andrews.ac.uk/prospectus

Applicants must state whether they prefer to transfer to Manchester or another Scottish medical school (approximately 50% to Glasgow, 30% to Edinburgh, 10% to Aberdeen and 10% to Dundee) at the end of the pre-clinical phase (Year 3).

Key contact

Dr David Jackson – admissions@st-andrews.ac.uk
Director of Medical Applications

St George's

5-year MB BS (A100)
www.sgul.ac.uk/undergraduate/mbbs-5-year-course

4-year MB BS Graduate Stream (A101)
www.sgul.ac.uk/undergraduate/MBBS%20Graduate%20Stream

6-year MB BS Foundation (A103)
www.sgul.ac.uk/undergraduate/foundation-for-medicine
www.kingston.ac.uk/medicinefdn

Key contact
Michilla Regan – mregan@sgul.ac.uk
Admissions Officer

Swansea

4-year MB BCh (A101)
www.gemedicine.swan.ac.uk

Key contacts
Dr Sarah Rees – s.g.rees@swansea.ac.uk
Admissions Tutor
Dr Adrian Evans – p.a.evans@swansea.ac.uk
Admissions Tutor
Clare Cowell – medicine@swansea.ac.uk
Admissions Coordinator

UCL (Royal Free and University College/RUMS)

6-year MB BS + BSc (A100)
www.ucl.ac.uk/medicalschool/mbbs-admissions

Key contact
Dr Brenda Cross – b.cross@ucl.ac.uk
Admissions Tutor

Warwick

4-year MB ChB Graduate Entry (A101)
www2.warwick.ac.uk/fac/med/study/ugr

Key contact

Ann Malczewski – A.C.Malczewski@warwick.ac.uk
Admissions Assistant

5 Working collectively /oridiv. activitles.

With Samir Matloob

Teamwork plays a crucial role in medicine, not only in patient care, but also in the personal and professional development of health-care professionals. In our experience, students and doctors who work collaboratively with others are often much more successful than those who are zealously ultra-competitive and isolated.

You should also strongly consider working collectively when applying for medical school. Working with other students who are in the same boat as you means that you will each improve your chances of getting the places that you want. By being creative and willing to work for each other, you can make the process less dull and overbearing and more inspiring and interesting.

If there are other students at your school or college who are also considering applying for medicine, you should think about setting up a 'medicine society' (if there isn't one already). It is a good idea to have a staff member to supervise the society. This may be the careers adviser or head of science. If there are only a few of you, speak to the principal to see if he or she can arrange for you to set the group up with students at other local schools and colleges so that there is a sizeable number. You could arrange to meet each week or fortnight to delegate responsibilities. As well as being a useful exercise, your initiative will impress your UCAS referee and the admissions panel.

There are a number of different activities that you can arrange for your regular meetings. A few suggestions are given below.

Guest lectures

You could invite the admissions tutor from a nearby medical school to speak about enhancing your applications. This can give you valuable insight into how admissions panels work and what they are looking for, as well as the opportunity to ask questions face to face. If you have a draft of your personal statement, you can be cheeky and ask them to have a quick look to give you some early feedback, if they are comfortable doing so.

In addition, you could invite doctors and medical students to give talks about their careers and own experiences of the admissions process. They can fill you in on the realities of the career and you can establish useful contacts who may be willing to guide you with your personal statements and interviews.

Journal club

Many medical departments hold regular 'journal clubs'. The aim is for junior doctors to review an article for a medical journal and critically appraise it for its usefulness and applicability to clinical practice. However, as you may be asked in interviews whether you read any medical literature, this can be a good way of everyone getting to grips with summarizing a paper and explaining the take-home message succinctly. Such an activity would also be impressive because it demonstrates a spirit of enquiry and early evidence of commitment to professional development.

You should encourage your school or college library to subscribe to some leading medical journals such as the *British Medical Journal* (*BMJ*), *The Lancet* or the *New England Journal of Medicine* (*N Engl J Med*), as well as the *Student BMJ*. Although these are high-impact journals, because of their wide readership they often have interesting articles and research papers that are not too difficult to get the gist of. Each week, a different student can prepare an article that he or she found of interest and present it to the rest of the group. Having the pressure of presenting to your peers will hopefully mean that you will be thorough in your analysis, and your general knowledge on medical issues will greatly improve, along with your presentation skills.

As well as new developments in the medical literature, you should also keep abreast of topical health issues receiving media coverage. These are the kind of issues that may be addressed in interviews. A different student can perform a news round-up each week of the latest areas of interest. You can use Newsnow, a free portal that can direct you to the latest news by the mainstream media both in and outside the UK. For up-to-date health news, see www.newsnow.org/h/Current+Affairs/Health. This also reduces the need to buy hard copies of newspapers every day (which can add to your cost of preparation).

In addition to presenting papers, you could also present reviews of popular medical books. There are some excellent books ranging from the history of medicine and biographies to controversial current affairs. Some books that are particularly good or relevant are listed in Chapter 11. Hopefully, these books will keep you interested and spark some debate on important topics, which can only enhance your critical thinking skills.

Similarly, important medical issues are often also portrayed on film (see the list in Chapter 11) and you may be able to screen some of these to watch together. These can prompt key discussions and may encourage you to find out more, particularly from a sociopolitical perspective.

Revision sessions

As you will all need to aim high in your exams, you can learn collectively too. You can arrange revision sessions in subjects such as biology and chemistry which most of you will be studying. For instance, each of you can concentrate on a particular area, which you can explain to your colleagues. Revising in a group can be motivating because you are being relied on by your peers. However, you should all be working constructively towards the same goals and it is essential that everyone is mature enough not to cause disruption.

Teaching/mentoring

As teaching and providing guidance to juniors is an important aspect of medicine, you can demonstrate your skills at an early stage. You can organize a mentoring programme where prospective medical students supervise GCSE candidates in a particular subject or with their revision as a whole. This can be both challenging and rewarding, and demonstrates your responsibility, maturity, leadership and teaching skills.

Similarly, once you move into Year 13, you can guide students entering Year 12 who are also keen on a career in medicine. This will establish continuity to any 'medical' society that you set up and make it a successful achievement for the long term.

Visiting medical schools

If a number of you are interested in visiting a particular medical school, you might want to arrange a group visit. If the medical school is happy to provide this outside the hustle and bustle of an open day, you can have more time to speak to admissions staff as well as students, and get a real feel for the medical school and its surroundings.

Getting into medical school together!

You can split into small groups where you review each other's personal statements. You should provide constructive feedback, which you are all prepared to take on board willingly and consider. However, you are warned against plagiarizing each other's statements, as this will be caught on the UCAS Copycatch software and you risk facing a reprimand (see Chapter 9).

Once the UCAS forms have been submitted, you will hopefully each receive some invitations for interview. When these come around, you can rally around to support each other by arranging mock interviews. Mock interviewing can be just as helpful to the interviewer as it can to the interviewee because it gives you an idea of what it feels like to be at the other end of the table and gauge what is expected of a candidate. After each interview, you can each report back on what questions were asked as well as details about the atmosphere at the different medical schools. This feedback will be useful for preparing for the big day when the opportunity comes around for others.

As long as each person is happy to do so, you may choose to update each other on the progress of your applications. Each offer can then be celebrated as a group and can motivate the remaining students to perform strongly at their interviews.

Making it work

The suggestions put forward above are merely ideas. There is no doubt that you can come up with more creative or relevant ones of your own that can enrich your own collective progress. The important thing is to be independent – identify your own needs and cater to them as a team. As we stressed earlier, the idea behind working together is that you are better motivated and interested in the world of medicine – something that will be clear at interviews as you speak with confidence and passion.

However, to really make it work, leadership is required. You can never have too many leaders as long as you all have each other's respect, though there are often individuals who just don't appear to be on the same wavelength. As a leader yourself, you should ensure that everybody feels at ease within the group, and listen to their needs and concerns. It is often the case that those who fail to contribute do so not out of laziness, but because they feel marginalized or lack a sense of belonging to inspire them. A good leader identifies this early, finds common ground and provides the necessary encouragement to bring out the best in each individual. Bear this in mind at all times to make your collective preparations successful and to ensure that each and every one of you is a successful candidate.

panel what is expected of a candidate. After each interview, you [illegible] each other back on what questions were asked as well as [illegible] about the atmosphere at the different medical schools. This feedback will be useful for preparing for the big day when the opportunity comes around for others.

As long as each person is happy to do so, you may choose to update each other on the progress of your application. Each offer can then be celebrated as a group and can motivate the remaining students to perform strongly at their interviews.

Making it work

The suggestions put forward above are merely ideas. There is no doubt that [illegible] points of view [illegible] your [illegible] process. The important thing is to be independent [illegible] [illegible] [illegible] [illegible] [illegible] speak with confidence and [illegible]. In this chapter, we:

[illegible]

[illegible]

[illegible] and [illegible] [illegible] the [illegible] to make your [illegible] performance successful and to [illegible] [illegible] and [illegible].

6 Demonstrating your qualities

The purpose of your personal statement and interview is to show the medical schools whether or not you are going to be a good doctor based on your academic and non-academic achievements. To be able to convince sceptical referees and interviewers in 47 lines and 15 minutes requires strong insight into what they're looking for, as well as personal insight.

In this chapter, we:

- guide you through the desirable qualities in doctors
- give you a few ideas on how you can gain experiences that reflect these qualities in you.

Ideally, you are reading this chapter at least a year before you are due to apply. If not, we hope it will help you put some perspective on your experiences and achievements thus far.

Later on in the book, we go through how you can express your experiences in your personal statement and interviews.

What is a good doctor?

Everyone – be they patient, politician, journalist, academic, nurse or, of course, doctor – has their own answer to this question. Some favour certain qualities over others, but by demonstrating that you are a well-rounded person you will not fall short on too many people's expectations.

The following is a list of personal qualities and skills that are often associated with good doctors:

- Caring and compassionate
- Committed
- Good communication skills
- Honest
- Initiative
- Leadership
- Organized
- Responsible
- Respect for confidentiality
- Spirit of enquiry
- Team player
- Teaching.

Actions speak louder than the words

It is not unusual in personal statements to see applicants listing these qualities and skills about themselves. However, this alone does not score many points, because it merely demonstrates awareness of qualities without backing them up with experiences and achievements. In reality, many candidates have very impressive experiences, yet failure to put these into the correct context can mean that they do not get the credit that they could.

What are the right things to do?

We would recommend a number of different areas in which you can act in order to check all the necessary boxes. Try to focus on ONE activity for each of the following areas. The important thing is that you enjoy the activities that you choose and that you are committed to them.

Voluntary work

Voluntary work, either in a hospital or with a residential care provider, is an excellent opportunity to gain skills and demonstrate your personal qualities, specifically:

- care and compassion
- good communication skills
- respect for confidentiality.

There is much more to be gained from work that involves interaction with patients or service users than clerical or administrative roles. Opportunities can be difficult to come by, but it is worth contacting the voluntary services department at your local NHS trust or council or looking through the *Yellow Pages* for residential homes and hospices.

To make your experience as fulfilling as possible, get involved as much as you can and use your initiative to help out the staff if there is anything else to do. It can also be very gratifying to take time to befriend patients so that you can build up confidence in communication, as well as enhance your understanding of how their illnesses or disabilities affect their lives. All of this will help in your interviews, where you will be able to speak with confidence and passion about the work that you have done.

Extracurricular activities

If you are not yet involved in any extracurricular activities, now is the time to start. If you are, try to get more involved (as long as it doesn't impinge on your studies). These activities are more impressive if they involve working with other people or if they demonstrate your organizational and leadership commitments.

For example, if you are a member of a sports team or a music group, get involved in organizing practice or gigs, introducing the activity to other students or arranging team-building trips, as well as pushing yourself to improve as an individual. Maintaining such commitments around a difficult academic schedule shows good organizational skills and effective time management.

Starting up your own society or group at school or in the community can also be a great way to acquire leadership skills and demonstrate initiative. Think about something that you and others would find enjoyable and helpful. As mentioned in Chapter 5, one idea is to set up a medical society with any other students interested in applying for medicine; such a society can arrange talks on medical careers and the application process, organize trips to open days at various medical schools, and create links with the local hospitals so that work experience and voluntary work can be easily obtained. By involving other people as much as possible, you can create a positive environment from which everyone can benefit. Being a doctor is never a one-person show and showing that you are capable of working positively with others to achieve your goals is a good sign.

Teaching

It is often forgotten that doctors have a responsibility to teach other doctors, students and healthcare professionals. Teaching requires dedication and commitment, but it can improve your communication and interpersonal skills significantly. It requires you to adapt to learning needs and styles that may be very different to your own.

You can demonstrate an interest in teaching and education by arranging collective revision sessions with other students. For instance, each person could work on a different topic and you could come together to teach each other what you've learnt. Alternatively, if you are feeling more confident than some of your peers, you could arrange to go through topics with them to bring them up to speed. Learning with your peers is one of the best ways of reinforcing and clarifying your own knowledge.

Spirit of enquiry

Doctors are also expected to continue their learning throughout their careers and carry out research. You can demonstrate your inquisitive personality by reading around developments in medicine in newspapers (such as www.independent.co.uk) and journals (such as the *BMJ*). The more carefully you read, the better your mind becomes at being able to think critically about the messages that the articles are attempting to convey.

Again, you can apply collectivism to this by starting up a journal club (see Chapter 5). You could take the lead in encouraging your school or college to subscribe to these publications for pupils to have access to. Each student could then read up one article each week and summarize it to the rest of the group at a meeting. Journal clubs are a mandatory educational activity for doctors, and there is no doubt that starting a voluntary one for sixth formers will impress admissions referees.

Come up with a plan

Make sure that you think about each of the personal qualities and areas of action individually, and come up with a plan to fill in any gaps in your own experiences. The suggestions that we have given are merely food for thought and no doubt you can come up with more personalized ideas of your own – just remember that they need to be both enjoyable and beneficial!

7 Work experience

With Yousef Basma

Not only is good work experience an essential component of your application, it is also the best way of evaluating whether a career in medicine is right for you. In your mind, you may not be able to look beyond becoming a doctor, but it is only after seeing what the work entails that the realities of the career truly sink in.

Indeed, good work experience has succeeded in putting many students off medicine in the past; some couldn't see themselves deriving satisfaction from the job or didn't enjoy being around sick people. For others, it was all too gory. These reactions are all understandable, and it is better to change your mind before you apply than when you are deep into your career.

What is work experience?

'Work experience' is an umbrella term, and students are often understandably confused about what counts and what doesn't. Put simply, it encompasses any clinical activity, whether voluntary or paid, that will improve your insight into a medical career. Any opportunity that fulfils this criterion is good enough, be it a rural general practice, a large urban teaching hospital or an overseas refugee camp.

How much work experience do you need?

To cover all your bases, you should aim to do the following:

1. Obtain a breadth of work experience encompassing medicine both in the hospital and in the community
2. Have a regular voluntary job based in a clinical setting, which will allow you to demonstrate your qualities and make an active contribution.

The importance and value of work experience

For admissions panels, work experience placements form a crucial part of assessing an applicant's suitability for medicine. Placements can be used to illustrate a wide range of your personal qualities that are sought after in a good doctor, including:

- an ability to balance commitments
- an understanding of teamwork – as well as getting involved yourself, you can observe how a team works in the clinical setting
- an appreciation of the communication skills required of a doctor
- a thorough awareness of the realities of medicine and the NHS
- a caring and compassionate nature.

How much work experience is needed?

Although all medical schools ask for evidence of work experience, there are no exact requirements. This works to your advantage because you can tailor your work experience to your needs. You should aim to cover the breadth that we alluded to above, but what will really count is your ability to *reflect* on your experiences in your personal statement and in your interview. Therefore, the more you have to draw from, the more you will have to say. Try to fit your work experience placements comfortably among your other plans and commitments, but aim for at least 1–2 weeks in hospital and general practice and a permanent voluntary job to which you will devote a couple of hours each week.

Hospital placements

The most important place to secure work experience is in the hospital. Regardless of where you want to end up in your career, most of the time spent in medical school and postgraduate training will be in the hospital environment.

You should avoid specialist hospitals and aim to undertake your placement at a teaching hospital or a district general hospital (DGH). These hospitals provide a wider range of services.

In terms of departments, it is best to stick to what medical students do most:

- General medicine:
    - cardiology
    - care of the elderly
    - endocrinology and diabetes
    - gastroenterology
    - neurology
    - renal medicine
    - respiratory medicine
- Paediatric medicine
- General surgery:
    - breast
    - colorectal
    - endocrine
    - upper gastrointestinal
    - transplantation
    - vascular
- Surgical specialties:
    - cardiothoracic surgery
    - ear, nose and throat
    - neurosurgery
    - oral and maxillofacial surgery
    - paediatric surgery
    - plastic surgery and burns
    - trauma and orthopaedics
    - urology.

It is not advisable to do a placement in obstetrics and gynaecology, because some patients may not consent to your presence, which can result in a lot of waiting around.

On a placement in one of these departments, you will gain a broad understanding through:

- shadowing junior doctors on the ward
- ward rounds
- outpatient clinics
- multidisciplinary team (MDT) meetings
- radiology/histopathology meetings.

If you undertake a medical attachment, you are also likely to see doctors perform procedures such as angiography, bronchoscopy or endoscopy (depending on the specialty). In surgical attachments, you may be able to go to theatre and watch operations. You should also take up any opportunities to visit the intensive care unit (ICU) and the accident and emergency department (A&E).

During term time, you are also likely to come across medical students and may be able to join them on their teaching sessions.

Community placements

Primary care plays an integral part in the NHS and increasingly more so. A placement in general practice will provide you with an insight into community-based medicine. Although often busy places, they may be able to offer you better 'one-to-one' exposure with doctors and other health-care professionals.

In a general practice placement, you will be able to sit in on clinics with doctors and nurses and go on home visits, as well as appreciate how the practice is managed behind the scenes. You may also be able to shadow or meet other primary care health professionals such as district nurses, health visitors, smoking cessation advisers and social workers.

Psychiatry placements

If you have a particular interest in psychiatry, by all means you should try to gain some experience in this area. Psychiatry is different in many ways to other specialties. In order to cause as minimal disruption as possible to patients' lives, much of the care is now provided in the community in addition to hospital mental health units. You will see that psychiatrists work very closely with a wide range of other professionals such as community psychiatric nurses, social workers and substance misuse counsellors, and that they rely heavily on their communication skills because there are often no definitive diagnostic tests to aid their practice.

In a psychiatry placement, you may be expected to go to various community sites as well as the hospital. You will be able to attend ward rounds, clinics, MDT meetings and possibly electroconvulsive therapy (ECT) sessions.

On your first day, it is imperative that you are given a thorough induction on ward practice and conduct by the consultant or senior nurse. Although it is rare for staff to encounter danger, some patients, in their altered mental state, may become hostile or distressed. It is important that you are aware of any necessary precautions and that you are able to remain calm.

Obtaining placements

Despite the importance of work experience, NHS bureaucracy can make arranging placements quite difficult. However, with some creativity, persistence and good organization, you can manoeuvre your way around this to ensure you do not miss out. You need to give yourself good time though, and start as early as possible, even a year in advance.

Find out about good hospital placements

Speak to your friends at school or college, students from older year groups and your teachers for advice on work experience. Your school or college may have established links with certain hospitals, but you should vet these by speaking to students who may have been on one of these attachments in the past.

Alternatively, if you attend an open day or taster course at the medical school associated with your local hospitals, ask the medical students there if there are any consultants with whom they would recommend you undertake your work experience. There is also a 'work experience' forum on www.admissionsforum. net where you may be able to find some valuable advice and recommendations.

Contacting your local hospitals

- Go to the NHS Choices website (www.nhs.uk)
- Find your local hospitals by entering your post code into the 'Hospital search' form
- Identify a suitable hospital
- Phone the hospital switchboard and ask to speak with the human resources department (the safest bet is to try in the morning – avoid phoning at lunch time)
- Introduce yourself and tell them that you would like to undertake a work experience placement at the hospital and if they could advise you on how you can go about this
- If there is an application process, ask them to send you the details and forms by email
- Ask politely for the person's name, direct number and email address
- Follow the instructions and return any signed forms by post
- If you do not hear from them after 2–3 weeks, chase up the person you contacted and keep doing so until you get an answer.

In every form of correspondence, be it by telephone, email or post, it is important to remain polite and professional, yet be persistent.

Sneaking in through the back door

If placements cannot be arranged through trust administration, you should contact consultants directly. Although this may be hit and miss, the chances are that any consultant who does respond is likely to show interest and will try his or her best to make the placement worthwhile.

On most trust websites, you should be able to find lists of consultants within each department. Choose one of the consultants from a department that seems most appealing to you (see above). Some sites will also have contact details, whereas those for others can be found elsewhere (sometimes in an area titled 'For GPs'). In any case, it is likely that their email address will be firstname.secondname@trustname.nhs.uk, or you may be able to find it through a Google search. Send them an email along the lines in the box.

From: johnh@tearguts.co.uk

To: Percival.Pott@bartsandthelondon.nhs.uk

Subject: Work experience placement

Dear Mr Pott,

I am a student currently working towards my GCSEs. I am very interested in a career in medicine and would like to undertake a 2-week work experience placement at St Bartholomew's Hospital during my summer holiday (from 29 June to 7 September). Would it be possible for me to do this under your supervision?

I would be grateful if you could advise me on how I can go about arranging this. If this is not possible, are there any alternatives you would be able to suggest?

Thank you for your time.

Yours sincerely,

John Hunter

Give consultants a few days to reply. If they do not get back to you, give their secretaries a call via the hospital switchboard and explain the situation to them. At the same time, you should hedge your bets by applying to a number of different hospitals and consultants. Someone out there will be willing to give you the opportunity that you deserve!

GP placements

Obtaining a GP placement can often be as difficult as finding a hospital placement. Again, it requires advanced planning and persistence. You can find local GPs the same way as hospitals on the NHS Choices website. However, this time, ask to speak to the practice manager.

 Ensure that you clarify with the practice manager that your placement will be supervised by doctors. Sometimes, students are left short-changed when they are told that they are not allowed into consultations and are left to do clerical duties. Although these may be valuable experiences, during a work experience placement you want to see as much as possible from the doctor's perspective.

Psychiatry placements

A list of useful contacts for work experience placements can be found at www.rcpsych.ac.uk/training/careersinpsychiatry/careerinfoforschoolleavers.aspx.

If none of these is close to where you live, you will be able to find your local mental health NHS trust at www.nhs.uk/servicedirectories/Pages/MentalHealthTrustListing.aspx. You can apply the same methods as you would when trying to secure a hospital placement either through administrators or through a consultant.

Gaining the most out of your placement

Once your placement has been confirmed, it is important to maintain contact with your consultant supervisor via email. Ask them for any details of timetables, inductions, dress code and what you will need to bring with you. You should also arrange that, on your last day, you have time allocated to evaluate the placement with your supervisor. Send them another email around 2 weeks before you are due to arrive, reminding them and clarifying any details about which you are unsure.

Dress code

You will be entering a setting in which high standards of professionalism are expected. As such, you should dress smartly while remaining comfortable enough to be on your feet all day. Suits are therefore not required.

Muck in

Once you are on placement, try to get your hands dirty. This may mean helping junior doctors with their ward duties, passing messages between staff members, helping theatre staff set up the patients, and preparing the clinic room for the next patient. As well as ensuring that you don't get bored, this will be well received by the staff, who will be more inclined to take an interest and be keen to offer you help.

Get advice

It is understandable that you might be nervous being on a placement for the first time. If you are a GCSE or A-level student, you are likely to be considerably younger than the rest of the staff. However, this will not make any difference as long as you appear responsible and mature. Introduce yourself to all the different members of staff whom you come across (not just doctors) and explain to them why you are doing the placement and what you want to gain. If any questions pop into your head, or if there's anything that you think they can help you understand, do not hesitate to ask at an appropriate time. As well as being informative, this can help you build rapport and be at ease.

If you want further advice about medical schools and the admissions procedure, it is a good idea to speak to junior doctors and medical students about their experiences. If anybody whom you come across is particularly helpful, ask them if you can keep in contact and if they would be willing to help in the future with your personal statement and interview preparations.

Be observant

You should study closely the relationships between staff and patients. Take into account the different communication techniques that staff members use in order to make patients feel at ease, listen to their concerns and give them advice. You may find good and bad examples, and this can help you appreciate the importance of good communication skills in clinical practice for yourself.

Also consider the multidisciplinary involvement in the care of different patients. This can be brought to light by ward rounds and MDT meetings, where the holistic approach to patient care becomes apparent. Doctors need to demonstrate strong team working and leadership skills, and you will see the importance of good interdisciplinary communication in being able to provide optimal holistic care.

Keeping a record

It is a good idea to keep a diary of everything that you see on your placements. You may wish to jot things down in a notebook during the day, which can be written up in the evening. This provides you with a means of reflection and you can refer to the Internet if you wish to find out further information. A placement diary can be added to your portfolio which can serve to refresh your memory when you are writing your personal statement and preparing for interviews. You should also show it to your UCAS referee.

At the end of your placements

When you began your placement, you should have arranged that on your last day you would be scheduled to have an evaluation session with the consultant. This is a good place for you to thank him or her, provide any feedback and ask any final questions. You may also print out and show the consultant your placement diary and clarify any points about which you were unsure. Considering that much of your time may have been spent with junior doctors and other members of the MDT, the consultant will be impressed by your professionalism and your endeavour.

It is essential that you ask the consultant if he or she can write you a reference for your portfolio. Ask when he or she will be able to provide this and remember to keep badgering him or her (politely) for it if it doesn't come. A copy of this should be given to the person writing your UCAS reference.

Voluntary work

Voluntary work demonstrates commitment, a caring nature and good time management. As far as the admission procedure is concerned, the best placements are those that involve interaction with patients or service users. Many hospitals are able to arrange volunteering placements on hospital wards where you will be required to help out nurses and speak to patients. Try to devote a few hours each week in the evening after school, during your free periods or at the weekend. Alternatively, you can try to arrange a placement in a residential home or with disabled people, which will give you similar exposure.

To arrange a volunteering placement, you should contact the volunteering department at your local hospital and enquire about any available positions for 'ward volunteers'. Sometimes, the recruitment process is competitive and you may be invited for a group interview, where they will be looking to see that you have team working skills and are friendly.

Once you are allocated a placement, make sure that you put in effort and become a committed and valued team player. Hopefully, you will personally find it a rewarding experience and nurses and other staff will appreciate your hard work. You will find that your own communication skills will develop and that you will understand the pressures and the satisfaction of working in a health-care setting first hand. These sentiments will then come through strongly in your personal statement and your interview.

As with work experience placements, you must get a reference for your voluntary work before your UCAS reference is written; you should try to get this from the ward sister, who will be well aware of your commitment, your team working and communication skills, and your caring and compassionate nature. Keep chasing the person up for this and provide your UCAS referee with a copy.

Gap years

If you choose to take a gap year, the opportunities are endless. In addition to work experience placements in the UK, you can travel and undertake voluntary experience overseas, which will be looked at favourably by admissions panels. You will also need to work for part of the year to fund this, and it is possible to find a job as a health-care assistant or auxiliary nurse. Overall, in addition to demonstrating positive personal qualities, a gap year can be used to gain high levels of responsibility and maturity. It may also give you an opportunity to develop language skills from your A levels or learn a new language altogether.

The decision to take a gap year might be because of your own ambitions or through circumstance. If you intend on taking a gap year before entering medicine, you should apply through UCAS via a deferred entry and mention your plans on your personal statement with particular reference to what you hope to gain. However, some students take gap years because they achieve the required grades at A level but were unsuccessful in their UCAS applications and clearing. You should confirm your gap year plans with the universities to which you have applied so that they have suitable dates in which they can interview you if you are going to be out of the country for part of the year.

If you are planning ahead to take a gap year, you should balance the substantial personal gains against the costs. As well as being potentially expensive and a way of building up early debt, you may also see it as a year of lost income as a working doctor later in life.

There are plenty of organizations that provide opportunities for voluntary work, particularly in developing countries. However, you should always verify their suitability independently. You should also make sure that you have travel insurance (see www.moneysupermarket.com/travelinsurance/?source=MS) and visit your GP to ensure that you have taken all the necessary precautions for your own health. It is a good idea to travel with friends on whom you can rely, and you should plan as many details of your placement in advance as possible, especially your budget! There is a vast amount of information available online about almost every destination in the world, and there are also many relevant books worth having a look at.

8 Admissions tests

With Ahmed Aber and Susannah Love

With medical schools inundated with increasing numbers of applicants and little means of differentiating between them, the vast majority have now adopted entrance tests to assist them objectively in the selection process. These tests aim to be a robust and transparent adjunct to the pre-existing selection methods such as academic performance, personal statement and reference, and interview. They have been designed to test overall aptitude for a career in medicine, although some also test scientific knowledge.

There are three tests that are employed for selection by different medical schools for their different courses:

- UK Clinical Aptitude Test (UKCAT)
- Biomedical Admissions Test (BMAT)
- Graduate Australian Medical School Admissions Test (GAMSAT).

Table 8.1 identifies the tests used by the various medical schools in the UK.

Table 8.1 Tests used by medical schools in the UK

Medical school	Standard courses (5/6 years)	Graduate entry courses (4 years)	Foundation/ extended courses (6 years)
Aberdeen	UKCAT	n/a	n/a
Barts and the London	UKCAT	UKCAT	n/a
Birmingham	no test	no test	n/a
Brighton and Sussex	UKCAT	n/a	n/a
Bristol	no test	no test	no test
Cambridge	BMAT	(BMAT)[a]	n/a
Cardiff	UKCAT	n/a	UKCAT
Dundee	UKCAT	n/a	UKCAT
East Anglia	UKCAT	n/a	UKCAT
Edinburgh	UKCAT	n/a	n/a
Glasgow	UKCAT	n/a	n/a
Hull–York	UKCAT	n/a	n/a
Imperial	BMAT	UKCAT	n/a
Keele	UKCAT	GAMSAT	UKCAT
King's	UKCAT	UKCAT	UKCAT
Kingston	n/a	n/a	no test
Leeds	UKCAT	n/a	n/a
Leicester	UKCAT	UKCAT	n/a
Liverpool	no test	no test	n/a
Manchester	UKCAT	n/a	UKCAT
Newcastle	UKCAT	UKCAT	UKCAT
Nottingham	UKCAT	GAMSAT	n/a
Oxford	BMAT	UKCAT	n/a
Peninsula	UKCAT/GAMSAT[b]	n/a	n/a
Queen's (Belfast)	UKCAT	n/a	n/a
Sheffield	UKCAT	n/a	UKCAT
Southampton	UKCAT	no test	UKCAT
St Andrew's	UKCAT	n/a	n/a
St George's	UKCAT	GAMSAT	(see Kingston)
Swansea	n/a	GAMSAT	n/a
Warwick	n/a	UKCAT	n/a
UCL	BMAT	n/a	n/a

[a]You should contact Cambridge University and your preferred college in advance; they will advise you on whether the BMAT is required.

[b]If it has been over 2 years since you did your A levels, you will need to sit the GAMSAT.

UKCAT

www.ukcat.ac.uk

As Table 8.1 demonstrates, the most widely used admissions test by far is the UKCAT, which is taken by the vast majority of applicants. This test was introduced in 2006 as a collaboration between a consortium of medical schools and Pearson VUE, a company that specializes in computer-based cognitive testing. The UKCAT is a 2-hour examination that aims to test innate cognitive abilities, including problem-solving skills, logical reasoning, critical thinking, information management and professional behaviour. There is no curriculum.

There are five sections to the UKCAT:

1. Verbal reasoning
2. Quantitative reasoning
3. Abstract reasoning
4. Decision analysis
5. Non-cognitive analysis.

Each section is timed. The test is also available for students with documented special educational needs (UKCATSEN), who are allowed extra time to complete the sections.

Verbal reasoning

Time allowed:

22 minutes (UKCAT), including 1 minute for instructions
28 minutes (UKCATSEN)

This test examines your ability to derive the correct conclusions from written statements. A passage of text is followed by four statements relating to it. The task is to read each passage of text carefully and, using the information provided, decide whether or not the statements follow logically. For each statement, one of three options must be chosen:

True – the statement follows consistently from the passage
False – the statement is not consistent with the passage
Can't tell – it is not possible to decide, based on the information provided in the passage, whether the statement is true or false.

It is important to note that answers should be based only on the information provided in the text and *not on previous knowledge*. You need to apply your judgement to decide:

- If you are in a position to decide on the statement itself
- If you are, then decide whether it is true or false.

This subtest consists of 11 reading passages with 44 test items.

Quantitative reasoning

Time allowed:

22 minutes (UKCAT)
28 minutes (UKCATSEN)

This test examines your ability to solve numerical problems. You will be expected to use basic calculations to manipulate information that is presented in tables, charts and graphs. There are 10 presentations in total, each accompanied by 4 test items relating to each. For each of these 40 items, you need to choose the single best answer out of 5 options.

Abstract reasoning

Time allowed:

16 minutes (UKCAT), including 1 minute for instructions
20 minutes (UKCATSEN)

This test examines your ability to identify patterns and similarities in abstract shapes. This is a measure of fluid intelligence, which comprises the ability to learn innovative or new information. Items are presented in a diagrammatic form including irrelevant and distracting material.

For each part of this test, you will be presented with two sets of shapes (set A and set B). The shapes in each set are similar but the two sets are unrelated. You will need to allocate five isolated shapes into set A, set B or neither.

There are 13 pairs of sets with 65 test items.

Decision analysis

Time allowed:

30 minutes (UKCAT), including 1 minute for instructions
37 minutes (UKCATSEN)

This test assesses your ability to decipher and interpret coded information. You will be presented with a scenario with information contained within text and figures such as tables. There is a significant amount of information with progressively more complex issues. You will be given 26 items related to the scenario with a subsequent 4 or 5 response options. You will need to identify the correct options of which there can be more than one.

Non-cognitive analysis

Time allowed:

30 minutes

The aim of this test is to assess behavioural aptitude by objectively measuring personality traits such as empathy, integrity and mental robustness. Unlike the other sections, the result of this section is qualitative and is currently only being used for research purposes. This may change in the future if patterns are found to emerge in medical school performance. Some medical schools may also use the results in tailoring personal development needs of individual students.

You will be presented with a number of statements, and you need to state whether you strongly agree, agree, disagree or strongly disagree with these.

Examples of the results provided by the UKCAT practice tests include:

'You appear to balance being self-sufficient, discreet and happy to make your own decisions with being socially and emotionally engaged and outgoing.'

'You have a moderate tendency to be impulsive, to take most opportunities as they arise and to be quite emotional in your reactions to events'

When should you take the UKCAT?

The UKCAT should be taken the same year that you are applying. Testing usually runs from 7 July to 9 October at a number of test centres internationally, although registration begins on 1 May. It costs £75 for students in the EU and £95 for students outside the EU. There is a reduced price of £60 for students from the EU who take the test in July or August. You can book the test at www.pearsonvue.com/signin.

Preparing for UKCAT

There are conflicting views on the value of preparing for UKCAT. However, it is useful to become familiar with the format of questioning and perhaps even work out your own approaches. There are a limited number of practice questions for each section available at www.ukcat.ac.uk/pages/details.aspx?page=practice Questions.

In addition, several online commercial ventures have seized the opportunity to provide preparatory material, feedback and coaching. There are also an increasing number of preparatory books. It is a good idea to discuss these on forums such as www.admissionsforum.net or www.newmediamedicine.com/forum/ukcat and decide for yourself whether or not you feel that they are worthwhile.

Further reading

Bryan M and Clayden J. *How To Pass The UKCAT*. London: Kogan Page Ltd, 2009.

Green M and Jethwa J. *Succeeding in the 2009 UK Clinical Aptitude Test (UKCAT)*. Nottingham: Apply2 Ltd, 2009.

Osinowo T, Weerakkody R and Woodward H. *BMAT and UKCAT Uncovered*. London: Wiley-Blackwell, 2008.

Picard O, Tighlit S, Tighlit L and Phillips D. *600 UKCAT Practice Questions*. London: ISC Medical, 2009.

Taylor F, Hutton R and Hutton G. *Passing the UK Clinical Aptitude Test (UKCAT) and BMAT 2009*, 4th edn. Exeter: Learning Matters Ltd, 2009.

BMAT

www.bmat.org.uk

The BMAT is necessary for standard undergraduate applications to Cambridge, Imperial, Oxford and UCL medical schools. It may also be required by those applying for graduate entry at Cambridge.

The BMAT is taken on 4 November after your UCAS form has been submitted, but you must apply by 30 September for the reduced fee of £32.10 for UK candidates and £55.90 for international students. You may still apply up to 15 October, but the fees will increase to £64.20 and £110.80 respectively. Candidates usually take the BMAT at their school or college, although it can also be taken at private centres at additional cost.

The BMAT is made up of three papers:

Section 1: Aptitude and skills
Section 2: Scientific knowledge and applications
Section 3: Writing task.

The specification for the test can be found on the BMAT website.

Section 1: Aptitude and skills

Time allowed: 60 minutes

This paper is made up of multiple-choice and short-answer questions. There are three elements involved in this paper:

1. Problem-solving
2. Understanding argument
3. Data analysis and inference.

About 30 minutes should be spent on 'problem-solving', which will require the application of simple numerical and algebraic principles. The rest of the time should be split between the other two sections. 'Understanding argument' involves drawing conclusions to logical arguments, identifying reasons and detecting flaws. 'Data analysis and inference' requires data interpretation of verbal, statistical and graphical stimuli.

Section 2: Scientific knowledge and application

Time allowed: 30 minutes

This paper is also made up of multiple-choice and short-answer questions. You will be tested on knowledge and its application in biology, chemistry, physics and mathematics. The standard of knowledge required will be that of GCSE Double Science and Mathematics.

The BMAT specification has identified national curriculum areas that will **not** be tested:

- Green plants as organisms
- Useful products from metal ores and rocks
- Useful products from air
- Changes to the Earth and atmosphere
- The Earth and beyond
- Seismic waves.

Section 3: Writing task

Time allowed: 30 minutes

You will need to choose one task out of three options, which will be based on general, scientific or medical topics. Your response must be limited to one side of A4 paper. The examiners will be assessing whether you can express your arguments critically and with 'unimpeachable logic', and organize your thoughts in a concise and structured manner. This response may be used in your interview to trigger further discussion.

Preparation

You should try to get as much practice as possible with the types of questions that will come up in the BMAT. It is a good idea to freshen up your factual knowledge of GCSE science and mathematics, remembering important details such as physics formulae. There are a range of resources available on the BMAT website that can be used, as well as an official guidebook.

Like UKCAT, there are also companies offering access to practice material and guidance, but you should be careful before spending your money. You can find out more and take part in discussions with other students at www.newmediamedicine.com/forum/bmat.

Further reading

In addition to the books which combine guidance on UKCAT (see p. 98), there are other books that you may find helful:

Butterwoth J, et al. *Preparing for the BMAT: The official guide to the BioMedical Admissions Test.* Oxford: Heinemann Educational Publishers, 2005.

Tyreman C. *How to pass the BMAT: Unbeatable preparation for success in the BioMedical Admissions Test.* London: Kogan Page Ltd, 2009.

GAMSAT

www.gamsatuk.org

The GAMSAT was designed in Australia as a selection tool for their graduate programmes and it was adopted by the UK medical schools that pioneered such courses here. It is currently used for applicants to graduate entry courses at Keele, Nottingham, St George's and Swansea medical schools, as well as for entry onto the standard course at Peninsula Medical School if it has been over 2 years since you took your A levels. Unlike the UKCAT and BMAT, the GAMSAT requires basic scientific knowledge to first-year university level.

Three papers make up the GAMSAT:

1. Paper 1 – Reasoning in humanities and social sciences
2. Paper 2 – Written communication
3. Paper 3 – Reasoning in biological and physical sciences.

All three papers are sat on the same day, with 5½ hours of exam time with a 1-hour break. It is a written exam that can be taken at several locations in the UK in September of the year before entry to medical school and costs £195. The applicant is given a score for each section of the exam and an overall weighted score, which is used for interview short listing. To be successful, the applicant must pass each section. Medical schools select applicants in the top tier of scores (usually the top 15–25%) for interview.

Paper 1 – Reasoning in humanities and social sciences

This section is made up of 75 multiple-choice questions, consisting of a series of stimuli in the form of written passages, tables or visuals relating to sociocultural, personal and interpersonal topics. The paper is designed to test areas such as complex verbal processing, logical reasoning and critical thinking.

Paper 2 – Written communication

This paper involves two 30-minute writing tasks that are related to a specific theme:

1. Sociocultural issues
2. Personal and social issues.

Assessment is based on:

1. Thought and content
2. Organization and expression.

It is important to respond in a structured and relevant way to the task. The ideas and attitudes that you express are not themselves assessed.

Paper 3 – Reasoning in biological and physical sciences

This paper is made up of 110 multiple-choice questions. They involve a series of stimuli that may be written, visual, graphical or mathematical, and you will be expected to apply basic scientific skills such as data analysis and problem-solving. Questions will be based on biology (40%), chemistry (40%) and physics

(20%). The biology and chemistry questions may be up to first-year university level, whereas physics questions will be of A-level standard.

Preparing for GAMSAT

The first step to preparing for the GAMSAT is to download the GAMSAT guidance book from the GAMSAT UK website and buy the GAMSAT sample question books from the UCAS books website (£15 each for sample questions and practice questions; £25 for the practice test). This will enable you to acquaint yourself with the style of the exam, the standard of the questions, and identify the areas on which you will need to focus. It is also advisable to get a hold of some A-level science revision guides.

Non-science graduates

Several non-science graduates (particularly non-biological science) have been successful at GAMSAT. However, you may need to do further preparation using textbooks and revision guides. There are also preparation courses available but these can be expensive. If you are a current university student, you might seek some preparatory advice from a tutor in the biological sciences department.

The GAMSAT is a competitive and expensive exam and you need to perform to a very high standard on the day. You should assess yourself using the preparatory material and determine how much work you are going to need to do to get up to speed. If this is going to be unrealistic, you should recognize this early and apply to the graduate entry programmes not requiring GAMSAT.

(20%). The biology and chemistry questions may be up to first-year university level, whereas physics questions will be at A-level standard.

Preparing for GAMSAT

The first step in preparing for the GAMSAT is to download the GAMSAT guidance booklet from the GAMSAT UK website and buy the GAMSAT sample question books from the UCAS books website (£15 each for sample questions and practice questions; £45 for the practice test). This will enable you to acquaint yourself with the style of the exam, the standard of the questions and [illegible]

Non-science graduates

Several [illegible]

[illegible]

[illegible]. There are also [illegible] available, but [illegible]

[illegible]

The GAMSAT [illegible]

[illegible] work you are going to need to do to get up to speed [illegible] you should recognise that [illegible] to the study [illegible]

9 Perfecting your personal statement

With Gosagan Gopalakrishnan

Most candidates applying to medical school tend to meet the minimum entry requirements. Therefore, the personal statement on your UCAS form is your first real opportunity to show the admissions panels how much you want to study medicine and why you will make a good doctor. In this chapter, we give you a few ideas on how to write your personal statement, as well as briefly skimming through a few of the other less exciting bits on the UCAS form.

Think about starting your first draft approximately around the April before you apply. This is the appropriate time frame in which to produce a great personal statement. As this is during term time, it will also give teachers or lecturers plenty of time to review what you have done and give you constructive criticism. You should realize that this will be a fluid process and your statement is likely to change considerably by the time you get to the end-product.

For the 2009 entry, there were 18 805 applicants for medicine, so you can see that each admissions team will have thousands of UCAS forms to sift through. This means that most forms, including the personal statement, have only a few minutes to make an impression on the reader.

The biggest hurdle with all interviews is getting short listed and, at many medical schools, the personal statement is the deciding factor. It gives you a chance to demonstrate your qualities and express your commitment to the career – so it's worth spending some time to really nail it!

Write your statement like a '**PRO**'. Think about the following criteria when looking at each of your paragraphs:

Personal – relates to your experiences

Relevant – this is exactly what the medical school will be looking for

Original – don't leave out the bits that are going to make you stand out

Broadly speaking, the personal statement should cover each of the following areas:

1. Why you want to become a doctor
2. **The steps you have taken to find out more about the career (such as work experience)**
3. **Your academic pursuits and interests**
4. **Your personal qualities (cross-referenced to your extra-curricular activities and achievements)**
5. A summary of why you should be short listed for an interview and any career intentions or aspirations that you may have.

Some admissions tutors will have a checklist with some or all of these areas and will be reading your statement looking for examples.

The three areas in the middle (points 2–4) form the meat of your statement and are the most important parts – do not compromise the important content of these points if you are limited by words. However, aim to cushion them with a convincing introduction and summary that reflect your personality and your commitment to a medical career.

UCAS has a limit of 47 lines or 4000 characters in which to complete your personal statement. This gives you approximately one A4 sheet of size 12-point text, which should be more than enough for four or five good paragraphs. It is advisable to stick to prose, if only because you have little control over the formatting, and the version that UCAS sends to the admissions referees may not look as presentable as you would like.

The opening gambit

There is no fixed formula for your introductory paragraph, but saying 'you have always wanted to be a doctor ever since you grazed your knee' isn't going to cut the mustard. Different styles work for different people, but what's important is that you are comfortable with your approach and that it reflects your demeanour and personality. Some are keen to hook the admissions tutor from the outset with a catchy opening, whereas others prefer to keep it to the point. In this paragraph, you should aim to address 'why you want to be a doctor'.

Panellists are sceptical about students who 'want to help people' without qualifying the statement. One student who made this error on his statement was asked by an interviewer what his father's occupation was to which he replied, 'petrochemical engineer'. The interviewer then stated that his father probably helps more people than he does, as he only sees a few thousand patients a year, whereas a petrochemical engineer helps put petrol into the cars of hundreds of thousands. What is in your statement will often form the basis for your interview questions, so bear in mind how the content of your answers will play out face to face.

Example 1

One attention-grabbing method is to use a short anecdote of one of your experiences:

'"Quick call the crash team, Mr Y is unresponsive!" Dr Stenson yelled at no one in particular from the furthest bay on the ward. This was around the time as a Ward Volunteer at Broomfield Hospital when I was certain I wanted to study medicine. But it wasn't the adrenaline pumping, ER-style mêlée that ensued which reaffirmed my choice, but rather how team-centred the junior doctor's approach to this patient was and how each decision was based on deductive reasoning and a scientific basis.'

Example 2

For a more toned-down introduction, consider the approach that we use when answering the question in interviews in Chapter 10:

'My desire to study medicine stems from my passion for human biology and my enjoyment of working with people. The idea of solving patients' clinical problems using my knowledge and communication skills is very appealing to me. In order to explore this further, I work as a volunteer on the nephrology ward at Broomfield Hospital, where I have also been able to shadow junior and senior doctors. The element of hospital medicine that has attracted me the most is the teamwork approach that is at its heart, as well as the trust that doctors build with patients in a very short time and the responsibility that comes with it.'

The steps that you have taken to finding out more about the career

You should go into some depth about the experiences that you have had to prepare yourself for the career, because this not only shows that you are making an informed decision, but also reflects your commitment. You can include the length of any placements that you have done, particularly if, for example, you have been a volunteer over several months or years. If you are lacking in experience of a medical nature, you may be able to think of examples of how you acted in a caring role towards an elderly or infirm family member.

You can also mention any taster courses or careers fairs that you have attended, but remember to give an example of what you gained from it:

Example

'I attended the "Tasting Medicine" course at King's College London, where I was introduced to the rigours and the enjoyment of medical studies. I became aware of the importance of combining an understanding of the basic science with fine clinical skills to make a confident diagnosis. Moreover, I was able to meet doctors and medical students outside the clinical environment and ask them without the pressures of work or study about what the career entails and whether it had allowed them to fulfil their ambitions.'

The key trick in this paragraph is not the details, but your reflections on the experience and what it meant to you. You should aim to come across as an insightful and emotionally responsive person. There are further examples of this section later in this chapter when we consider exaggerations.

Your academic pursuits and interests

Your personal statement is not the place to talk about your grades – these will be there to see in the 'Education' section of your UCAS form. Your referee will also provide predicted grades. However, you can use your personal statement to talk about your achievements and work *beyond* the exam hall and the classroom with examples such as prizes. If you have undertaken any teaching or mentoring of other students, then this should be mentioned here too.

Example 1

'Last year I received the Biology Prize for my essay on 'Antibiotic resistance'. This was a proud achievement as it not only reflected the hard work that I had put in, but was also a great learning experience as I had to look beyond A-level textbooks and even refer to medical journals. At the same time, I had to make it an accessible and interesting read. I believe that this will be a useful experience as doctors are expected to write research or review papers that can be used to improve future research and practice.'

As discussed in Chapter 3, you can also refer to how you have personalized work in your A-level subjects according to your interests, which will come across as intelligent and pleasing. Of course, this means that you will need to know your stuff and be prepared for some questions in the interview, but, if these interests are genuine, why not?

Example 2

'I have a strong interest in psychology, which I developed during my AS-level course. I have been particularly drawn to neuropsychology and I gave a presentation to my college Science Society on the famous case of Phineas Gage. I have also read further into the subject through popular books by Steven Rose and Oliver Sachs and attended a psychiatric ward round where the consultant gave me an introduction into psychopathological signs. It has been apparent that the various aspects of psychology play an important role in neurology and psychiatry, specialties in medicine in which I have developed an early interest. However, I have also come to realize the important role that psychology plays in medicine as a whole, be it in the treatment of chronic illnesses or understanding health behaviours such as drug addiction.'

Your personal qualities

Your extracurricular activities and achievements can say a lot about the kind of person you are. In addition, they will make the admissions panel see what you have to offer to life at the university as a whole (for example, through sporting prowess or musical genius) and that you are able to strike a harmonious work–life balance.

You should mention here anything that you do at a reasonably high level, whether this is at school, such as debating or music, or outside school, such as a sporting interest for a club. You should also mention if you have done or are working towards a Duke of Edinburgh's award or ASDAN. But the secret is to emphasize the redeeming qualities (such as leadership or commitment) that you have gained or demonstrated through these activities (see Chapter 6).

Do not be shy about selling yourself! By putting your experiences and achievements in their correct context, they can be positive without sounding arrogant or overconfident.

Example 1

'This year I was crowned the World Tiddlywinks Champion, where I beat 11 competitors en route to the championship final. This victory is very special to me as it comes after 4 years of intense training to reach a mental and physical peak which will stand me in good stead for medical school.'

Impression:

Good at tiddlywinks

Committed

Example 2

'I am not particularly gifted at football but I love to play. Each week I look forward to playing as part of a seven-a-side team in a Sunday league and I relish the team spirit and camaraderie. Last season we finished in third place (a surprise result!) and I was presented with the team award for "most improved player". In the summer, I organized a team trip to a football camp where, as well as working on technical aspects of the game, we built on our team-working and leadership skills, which I realize are transferable to a career as a doctor.'

Impression:

Humble

Committed

Team player

Able to identify weaknesses

Initiative

Organized

Leader

Notice how Example 2, although less high achieving, is somehow more appealing to the reader. This is not because tiddlywinks is not glamorous, but rather that the second example says more about the author's personality and reflects many positive attributes of the modern doctor.

Sealing the deal!

The end of your statement should highlight anything else that you feel is important to your application and anything that you would like the admissions tutor to know about you. This might include details of any positions of responsibility that you have held, such as a school prefect or as the president of a society, or any prizes that you have won for your contributions.

This should be followed by a summation in which you give your 'mission statement' and leave the admissions tutor with a clear reason as to why they should pick you. This needs to deliver the killer blow to leave your readership in no doubt as to your commitment to a career in medicine. If you already have an inkling of the specialty in medicine that you intend to pursue then this is the appropriate place to mention it, but remember that it should be well founded and based on your work experience and further investigation. This is by no means mandatory – many medical students and Foundation doctors have little idea of where they will end up, let alone school leavers!

This information and the examples are intended to serve simply as a guide and not as firm rules set in stone. You do not necessarily

Example

'As a school prefect and through my voluntary work in the paired reading scheme, I feel a real sense of pride in my conduct and that it engenders in me a desire for a career in a position of responsibility such as medicine. I was pleasantly surprised recently when I was awarded the School Governor's Prize for the most outstanding contribution to the life of the school and felt a great sense of achievement, though I was a little embarrassed to have my efforts so publicly acknowledged!

'I truly believe that medicine captures all the elements of my interests and personality and provides a life-long vocation. As an intellectually rigorous and demanding course, I feel, as a motivated, enthusiastic and determined student, that I would be able to rise to the challenge and hope to one day become an asset to the medical profession.'

need to have six paragraphs – you can have more or less as you see fit. The best personal statements will lead naturally from one paragraph to the next without seeming like you are simply trying to tick all the boxes. You need to spend time drafting and re-drafting your statement until you feel that it is the best reflection of you as a person that you can put down on paper.

The fine print ...

Remember to check the UCAS website before drafting your personal statement as there is useful information to help you with your statement but, more importantly, it gives you the latest information on the length of the statement. In the 2009/2010 application cycle, UCAS only allowed 4000 characters, including spaces, which equates to roughly 600 words. This may not seem like a lot, but, if you stick to the key areas, and remove any superfluous language, you will be able to quickly trim your statement down.

Proofreading

Finally, when you are happy with your personal statement, get some sleep, wake up fresh and read it again. This may sound silly, but reading it over and over when you are tired can result in your mind playing tricks on you.

Use the spell-checker and grammar-checker on your word-processing software, but remember to make sure that it is set up with English (UK) and not English (US) as the default language.

Do not rely solely on the spell-checker, as this may not pick up all errors!

Once you are happy with your first draft, you need to have it reviewed by people around you. Give copies to your friends and family, and in particular show it to teachers, medical students and doctors. Ask them to give you constructive feedback and suggestions for development. Do not take offence if someone tells you that a paragraph is irrelevant but rather ask them what they are basing their opinions on and take their comments on board. Make any suggested changes and take it back to them to reread. Your teachers are an invaluable source of help and will have read many statements over the years – listen to what they have to say.

Plagiarism

Imagine that your friend in the year above you wrote a fantastic personal statement and got all four medical school offers. Rightly, you ask to see the personal statement to get an idea of what a medical school is looking for before drafting your own statement. You think that the form is brilliantly worded and incorporate certain phrases but change the order of some of the words and some of the specific details. Despite trying your best, some of it sounds quite similar to your friend's statement. You wanted to change it a bit more but ran out of time so submitted what you had.

This scenario is plausible and not entirely unreasonable. This is a difficult situation because this is considered plagiarism and it is something that UCAS and the universities have tried to clamp down on recently. In the 2009 application cycle, UCAS used a software programme called Copycatch, which compares your personal statement with a library of previously submitted applications, popular websites and some other materials, including books. This 'Similarity Detection Service' will flag up an application in which 10% or more of the content matches another, cleverly ignoring frequently used words such as 'and' and 'to' and text strings such as 'Duke of Edinburgh'.

If your application form is identified as suspicious, it is referred to a member of the UCAS Similarity Detection Service team, who verifies it and makes a decision on whether any further action, such as notifying the university, is required. If the university is notified, they will then decide on how to proceed with your application and may terminate it if there is sufficient evidence of plagiarism.

Make sure that your spelling, punctuation and grammar are correct. You will have already asked several people to check the content, but now you should get a teacher or a college tutor to read through your form simply from a grammatical stance to make sure none of these errors slips through. If you are invited to an interview, you will get a chance to make a good impression face to face, but, if a fussy interviewer notices a grammatical error such as *it's* instead of *its* then this can annoy them from the outset and make the interview even harder.

That little white lie and exaggerations ...

Can it really hurt your application if you bend the truth slightly in your personal statement? You may read over your statement and feel that it is a little inadequate or that you don't have enough experience. You may be tempted to fudge the truth slightly and suddenly that morning you spent in the local GP surgery with the receptionists becomes a 2-week placement with four of the partners! If you do lie on your UCAS form, you will probably come unstuck during your interview and be exposed as a fraud. Also it has been known for people to have an offer revoked because they were found to have been untruthful on their forms. The worst-case scenario is that your little white lie goes unnoticed during your admission stage but later comes to light at medical school, which could be disastrous and investigated as a probity issue that may result in your studies being terminated.

With the right spin on things and good reflection, you need not exaggerate and should not be tempted to do so! The morning that was spent with the receptionists can easily trump a 2-week placement on another form if it is contextualized and the learning points are exemplified.

When you have finished your personal statement, you can copy and paste onto your UCAS form. However, make sure that you always edit your work on a word processer, as the UCAS website will 'time out' after 35 minutes without saving your form, and you could end up losing your precious work!

Example 1

'Earlier this year, I was able to spend some time with receptionists at my local GP surgery and was able to see first-hand their role in coordinating the doctors' day and facilitating the smooth running of the practice. I gained an understanding of the telephone triage system and was able to appreciate the multidisciplinary approach to patient care with the other health professionals working at or out of the practice such as the physiotherapist, district and practice nurses, and the adjoining pharmacists.'

Example 2

'Recently, I spent 2 weeks with four partners at a GP surgery. I found this really useful as it gave me insight into the life of a doctor.'

We can see that, although the duration of experience and insight gained during the 2-week placement may have been more substantial, the half-day placement (Example 1) carries more weight here as it demonstrates a more genuine feeling of interest in a medical career.

Professional drafting services

You may come across companies that offer to proofread your personal statement, and some of these can even help with drafting it too. If you are thinking of using one of these companies, bear in mind that they will often use stock phrases and you could be caught out with the UCAS Copycatch checker even though you did not plagiarize anyone else's statement. Such services vary greatly in price, but could end up being a false economy if your application is withdrawn because of suspected plagiarism.

By investing some time and effort of your own and seeking advice from the people around you, you can come up with something more true to yourself and therefore better.

Mature students

If you are applying as a mature student, you should be honest about your motives for studying medicine and try to convey this in your personal statement. You will have a lot of life experience that a 17- or 18-year-old school leaver won't. Such experience should not be underestimated and you should express some examples of how this is transferable and relevant to a career in medicine.

Postgraduate applicants

Having decided to pursue another degree, you can take solace in the fact that you will probably find the whole application process a little less intimidating as you will have been through all of this during your first degree. You will probably be in a better position now as university life and life experience in general lend to a good personal statement. Whether you are applying during your first degree or after a PhD, you will still need to cover the same broad areas as a school leaver, though you should make it explicit that you are studying for or have completed another degree(s).

If you applied for a medical degree when you were at school but were unsuccessful, you will already have an idea about what is required and a base from which to start, and should not find yourself disadvantaged. Look carefully at your previous application and try to consider from an objective viewpoint why you might have been unsuccessful and how you can improve.

Some people say that a medical school will not reconsider an application from a candidate who has previously been rejected. This is hopefully the minority viewpoint, because most admissions panels will treat each application on its individual merits. In fact, stating that you have applied previously – if worded wisely – will demonstrate a commitment to medicine and admirable qualities such as dedication and perseverance.

If your degree is in a medically relevant field such as pharmacology or microbiology, you should make reference to how you feel that the course content has whet your appetite and prompted you to further your understanding in a more clinical or holistic environment. If your course is unrelated, such as French or aeronautical engineering, you should still make it clear that you have completed, or intend to complete, such a degree and make reference to the skills that this particular course has taught you which you feel may be beneficial to a doctor. So, if, for example, you are studying for a BA in French, you might comment on how, with medicine in mind, you have developed your general communication skills and, in particular, your active listening skills. You can also mention that you have taken an interest in medical French and have undertaken work experience in a health-care setting in a French-speaking country.

Overseas applicants

If you are applying as an overseas applicant, it is useful to remind the admissions tutors in a personal letter of your status, because they will have a number of places reserved for overseas applicants. Also, if you are being sponsored by your government to study medicine in the UK, you can make this clear in your personal statement towards the end, because it gives the reader a clear impression that you have already been assessed as a competitive candidate and demonstrates a further commitment to studying medicine as the sponsorship process may have already been lengthy.

It is probably worthwhile including a sentence or two in your personal statement that makes it clear that you are an overseas applicant. This can be done directly by stating that you are from country X or indirectly by including a city name that might be unfamiliar or foreign to the person reading your form. Doing this serves to intrigue your interviewers and can often break the ice at the start of your interview, because they may enquire about your journey and your country.

In particular, as an overseas applicant, you should say why you want to study at a UK medical school and state your level of proficiency in the English language. Although the advice given in this chapter about the statement as a whole will still apply, you must also make sure that your written English is perfect on your form. Some tutors/interviews, knowing that you are an overseas applicant, will make allowances for grammatical errors and certain turns of speech typical of the English spoken in various countries, but, as with a UK applicant, it is ideal to get the personal statement perfect.

If you are happy with the content of your personal statement but are unsure about the quality of your written English, take it to an English teacher at your school or college and ask them if they would kindly proofread if for you. You will find companies that offer a proofreading service, but these are often costly. If you are using one of these services, especially if they are a translation service, beware because they may substantially alter the gist of the points that you are trying to make.

Extenuating circumstances and special applications

If you are applying for medicine with extenuating circumstances – for example, you narrowly missed out on an offer and are reapplying or applying for the first time – or a personal event occurred that had an impact on your application or results previously, it is worth stating this on your form and the reasons surrounding it. Such a declaration fits best at the end of a personal statement in your summation paragraph and should be coupled with a purposeful adage on how you have spent your time since or what you gained from the experience. Be careful with how much information you divulge in relation to extenuating circumstances because sob stories in your personal statement may come across as a tad distasteful. Do not consider lying on the form about such matters, as you are likely to be caught out at the interview stage or later on in your career. Simultaneously, any explanation of your circumstances should be reiterated in your school or college's reference to UCAS (see below).

This idea is equally applicable if you have decided to take a gap year; that is, you should say that you are on a gap year, give your reasons for taking one, and expand on your experiences and what you have learnt.

Similarly, if you have special reasons for applying to a medical school in a particular region (such as family commitments), express this on your personal statement, because tutors are likely to be sympathetic to this fact.

Final thoughts

Above all else, remember that your personal statement is your first sales pitch in the application process and, at many medical schools, is the key to getting short listed for interview. Of the thousands of applications submitted, many students fail to be offered a single interview because they did not give enough thought to their personal statement or they failed to tick all the boxes. Don't underestimate the time required to produce the perfect statement and don't leave it to the last minute! What you must do is make sure that it reflects the best of you, that you are happy with it, and that it is an honest and glowing self-portrait.

There is a strong possibility that what you say in your statement will be discussed in further detail at the interview. Therefore, although the advice of others is invaluable, it is you who is going to have to face the music in the interview room. You need to make sure that you are going to be comfortable with the questions that they are likely to ask. Think long and hard about whether the statement really reflects you as a person.

The rest of the UCAS form – the less exciting bits

The UCAS application cycle begins on 1 September and all medical applications must be received by **15 October**. After this date, the medical schools have no obligation to consider your application. As long as you submit your application by the 15 October deadline, you will not be disadvantaged – there is no first-come first-served basis to the admissions process, so you can take your time, and be careful and considered.

The form must be completed online on www.ucas.co.uk. If you are applying through your school or college, they will inform you of a 'buzzword' which you must enter on the website when you register your application. This allows UCAS to link your application to your school or college so that they can provide you with a reference.

Try to complete this section as early as possible so that it is out of the way and you can focus your mind on perfecting the personal statement and concentrating on your studies.

Personal details

Student support

This relates to how you will be paying for your course. You need to make sure that you enter the correct fee code so that you avoid any unforeseen difficulties. Some of the relevant codes are:

01 – private finance – if you will be paying for the degree by yourself

02 – LA, SAAS, NIBd, EU, ChI, IoM or Student Finance England – most school leavers will need to pick this option; your fees will be covered by a government student loan

09 – overseas agency – if an overseas government or organization is paying for you.

Criminal convictions

You do not need to disclose any criminal convictions that have been 'spent', but bear in mind that the medical schools will ask you for a criminal record check, which may affect your eligibility for the course.

Disabilities/special needs

Make sure that you disclose anything that affects you (including dyslexia)

Additional information

This information is voluntary and does not need to be disclosed if you are uncomfortable about doing so. There are some compulsory questions:

Ethnic origin and national identity – there is the option of 'I prefer not to say'

Occupational background of your parents/guardian or yourself (if you are over 21) – you may write 'I prefer not to say'.

Choices

You are only allowed to make four choices for medicine (although you are allowed to make five choices overall). The form will automatically reject a fifth choice for a medical degree.

Some considerations:

- Make sure that you enter the correct course code; some medical schools offer conventional 5-year courses and 4-year accelerated graduate-entry programmes, so pick the right one for you.
- You may need to enter a campus code for some courses, for example:

    Barts and The London: all applicants should select Queen Mary University of London (Q50) as the institution code and then campus code Whitechapel (W)

    Cambridge: for the standard pre-clinical course, choose your preferred college or choose open application (9); you cannot apply to Homerton or Hughes Hall Colleges; for the 4-year graduate course you can choose from Hughes Hall (7), Wolfson (W), Lucy Cavendish (women only) (L) Colleges, or No preference (E)

    Imperial: for the 4-year graduate course select Hammersmith (H)

    Liverpool: for the 5-year standard course, choose to be based at Liverpool University (course code A100) or Lancaster University (A105)

    Newcastle: choose from Newcastle campus (N), Durham campus (D) or No preference (E)

Oxford: for the standard pre-clinical course, choose your preferred College of choice or choose Open application (9); you cannot apply to Harris Manchester or Mansfield Colleges; many of the Colleges also offer places on the 4-year science graduate programme

St Andrew's: choose where you want to undertake your clinical studies – Manchester (M), Scotland (S) for one of the other Scottish medical schools, or No preference (E)

- Enter the start date as when you intend on beginning your studies; if you are planning on deferring your entry, you should click on next year's date.
- Live at home? If you will be moving out of home and will require information about campus accommodation, check 'Yes'.

Should you apply for a non-medical course on UCAS?

On the UCAS form, students are able to apply for only four medical schools out of the five choices available to them. They are allowed to use the fifth choice for another subject in case they have no offers. There has been reassurance from UCAS that making a fifth choice will not put candidates at a disadvantage because medical schools will not be aware of it. However, it is likely that the additional course will be aware that you are applying for medicine from the tone of your personal statement and reference.

If you receive an offer in your non-medical choice, by choosing to accept, you will not be able to enter the clearing process. However, there are rarely any positions available at clearing in medicine anyway.

The choice therefore rests with you. If you intend on reapplying next year if you do not get any offers for medicine, there may be little point in putting down an additional choice. However, if there is another course that you would not mind doing, you have nothing to lose by applying for it.

Education

This section is tedious but extremely important.

1. Schools/colleges

You need to find the schools and colleges that you have attended and add them to your application.

2. Qualifications

You must enter details of:

- the qualifications that you have completed, including dates and awarding bodies – it is a good idea to have your results statements handy because they will have all the relevant information
- the qualifications that you are due to complete (e.g. A levels, International Baccalaureate or a degree)
- the admissions tests that you have taken (i.e. BMAT, GAMSAT and UKCAT).

Employment

Include the contact details of all of your previous employers – this is particularly relevant for graduates.

Reference

Your referee will need to fill out his or her details on your form. For school leavers, this should be your principal or another teacher. For graduates, it should be a university tutor, an employer or another relevant person.

Where you have pending grades, your referee is expected to provide predicted grades of how you are likely to perform. At many universities, these play an important role in the selection process, so you should try your best to ensure that you at least meet the minimum requirements at the schools to which you have applied. Obviously, the best barometer is your progress so far in your course. If you have been underperforming, you should approach your referee and broach the matter of predicted grades in a positive and mature manner. Reiterate the importance of the grades to your future, provide them with evidence of the steps that you have taken to turn things around this year and come up with a plan of action to improve.

Your referee should also give a perspective of your contribution to your college and your potential. It is a good idea, therefore, to have a meeting with your referee. Be sure to take a draft of your personal statement as well as your portfolio (see Chapter 1) with you. This should include your work experience diaries, any certificates or references that you have, and evidence of voluntary work and extracurricular activities. It is important that they become familiar with your drive and ambition, as well as your personal qualities and your experiences.

Waving goodbye to your UCAS form

After months of drafts and re-drafts, when you are happy with the final edit of your personal statement, it will be time to upload it on to the UCAS website and send it out into the ether. The easiest way is to copy and paste it into the personal statement window. Double-check that it has done this properly with no errors. Anything over 4000 characters won't make it, so check that you have not exceeded this and cut half your closing line off!

Once that's done, double-check the rest of the UCAS form and go through it with a fine toothcomb, making sure that there is nothing missing. You can look at the form in its entirety by clicking on 'View all details'. When you are happy with your form, save all of the sections and submit it!

Useful resources

www.ucas.ac.uk

www.newmediaMedicine.com/forum/personal-statements-ucas-forms

10 Mastering the interview

With Neil Soneji

Candidates often experience mixed feelings when they are called for interview – relief and elation, on the one hand, and nerves, on the other. However, if you are able to settle these and prepare well for the occasion, it is the perfect arena to sell yourself.

An invitation for interview itself is a good achievement because you are already likely to have jumped a number of hurdles to get one, including a good academic performance, the necessary predicted grades, an impressive personal statement and, possibly, a good showing in an entrance exam.

In this chapter, we give you some tips on how best to prepare for the interview, what kind of questions to expect and how to approach your answers.

Preparing for the big day

Primarily, it is important for you to have self-belief. You have come this far and you need to be determined not to let the opportunity pass. Be confident that you, your achievements, your communication skills, your knowledge and your critical thinking skills are going to brighten up that interview room and persuade those interviewers that you are the student they want!

Practice makes perfect. No matter how confident you are of yourself, it is advisable to get your thoughts together and rehearse the occasion with others. Make time with your friends or teachers to do mock interviews and encourage them to give honest feedback. If you remain in touch with any doctors or current medical students from your work experience or open days, see if they are available to practise with you too.

The best places to find question banks for each medical school are on internet forums such as New Media Medicine (www. newmediamedicine.com/forum) or AdmissionsForum.net (www. admissionsforum.net). Other candidates may also report their experiences from their interviews, which can also help you prepare.

Useful additional techniques include recording yourself on audio or video. This allows you to identify any faults of which you were not previously aware that you can address before the interview (for instance, in your posture or your tone of voice).

 If other students at your school or college have applied for medicine, form a group and agree to practise with each other whenever one of you is invited. This way, everyone grows accustomed to the format of interviews, each person can start thinking about good answers and those who have had interviews can share their experiences.

Tips for mock interviewers

1. If you are working from a question bank, you can always rephrase questions or throw in alternative but similar ones to encourage the candidate to think before answering.

2. Write down your honest and constructive feedback – pay particular note to the following:

   - Did the candidate communicate like a good doctor?
   - Has the candidate demonstrated that he or she has the qualities of good doctor?
   - Does the candidate understand what a career in medicine entails?
   - Is the candidate able to think critically about topical issues?

In the interview room

First impressions can be crucial and so it is important to be professional and confident from the outset.

Be friendly

The interviewers will introduce themselves with their names and what they do. Make sure that you smile politely and give them all a firm handshake, with a friendly comment such as 'nice to meet you' or 'how do you do?' This confidence will be well received. You will then be offered a seat; if not, ask politely if you may sit. A few comments or questions from the interviewers may follow to help you relax (for example, about your journey to the interview) before the questions begin in earnest.

Sitting posture

It is crucial to sit up straight and not slouch or lean over to one side. Rest your hands on your knees or your forearms on your lap and interlock your fingers in front of you so that you are in a position to gesture appropriately while answering. Be sure not to fidget. If there is a table between you and interviewers, you can rest your hands on it. Maintaining an attentive and confident posture is crucial because it ensures that the interviewers are engaged in what you say and not what you do.

Eye contact

This is pivotal in demonstrating both confidence and respect. It is advisable to maintain initial eye contact with the person who asked you the question while also addressing the others so that they too are engaged. Remember that some members of the panel may not utter a word during the interview but will be listening intently, so it is important that you do not shut them out.

Appropriate language

Slang should be avoided and medical terms can be used if appropriate and if you are confident of their meaning; you should be prepared to explain what you mean if asked.

Make use of 'power' verbs

As long as they are used in the correct context, these will bring your sentences to life and keep the interviewers engaged, for example, 'succeeded' instead of 'completed', 'negotiated' instead of 'discussed'.

Speech

The content of your answers should be delivered clearly and concisely; having structure will aid this (discussed in the next section). Pay attention to the tone of your voice, emphasizing certain words or phrases in your answer, as well as controlling the speed and inserting appropriate pauses. Make every word count and do not waffle – if it is not going to add anything to the quality of your answer, do not say it.

Approaching a question

- First, it is obviously important that you understand the question and answer it. It can be all too easy to regurgitate an answer that you have prepared to a *similar* question, without addressing what the interviewers have asked; do not fall into this trap. If you do not understand the question, it is acceptable to say so, and they may repeat it. You may ask them politely if they could rephrase the question (asking them to repeat it risks not understanding it a second time).
- Think before you speak! There is nothing wrong with a brief pause before setting off and this is better than diving into a poorly constructed answer.
- Structuring your answer should be at the top of your thoughts. Your answer should have a brief introduction, the main points

and then a brief summarizing sentence with a key point in it that you wish to make. By approaching the question from all angles, you will show that you have taken every aspect into consideration and weighed them up. You will also demonstrate that your thoughts are organized, which makes it easier for the interviewers to understand what you are saying and remain interested.

Content of answers

The aim of each answer is to sell yourself through your experiences and achievements, personal qualities, knowledge, communication skills and critical thinking skills, depending on the exact question. In this section, we look at a few common areas that are often covered in the interviews for which you would be wise to prepare.

To begin with, let us consider the two most common questions that are asked in interviews:

'Why do you want to study medicine?'

Candidates commonly take one of two approaches when answering this question. The first is to detail their enjoyment of science and caring for people; the second is to recount a personal experience (such as family illness) that inspired the candidate to pursue a career in medicine.

There is nothing wrong with taking either of these approaches or even using both, but you need to support your case as robustly and as personally as possible to make an impact. You should explain **how you explored the career further** and **what potentially makes you a good doctor**. Without these elements, your answer will be one-dimensional and unconvincing.

Consider layering your answer as shown in the box.

1. **Why you were motivated to consider a career in medicine in the first place**

   This can include one or both of the approaches above:

   A duty to help people – medicine involves helping people in need by combining scientific knowledge and strong communication skills.

   An interest in science – medicine involves solving problems by investigating patients' symptoms to diagnose and treat them.

   An interest in research – medicine is a permanently evolving science and there is potential to contribute by becoming an expert in a specialized area and carrying out research.

   A personal experience might open your eyes to a career in medicine, but this requires further justification about how you followed this up (see below).

2. **How you explored the career and what attracted you**

   Here you can incorporate any motivations that you discovered during work experience, voluntary work, taster courses or your studies.

   Doctors are always working with people – with patients and their families, as well as in a team with colleagues from a variety of professions.

   Doctors build an unparalleled trust and rapport with patients, and with that comes profound responsibility.

   Doctors are active teachers who are required to train juniors in everything from facts about diseases to hands-on practical skills.

   Health care in the broader context – here you can talk about how your interest in medicine was enhanced by your 'other' A-level choice because it allowed you to think about health care with a different perspective.

3. **What is going to make you a good doctor**

   You can round up your answer by making it clear to the interviewers what will make you a good doctor:

   You have a **proven academic track record** driven by an enquiring mind and a willingness to learn.

   You have **good communication skills**, which you have improved through your voluntary work; this will allow you to earn the trust of your patients and to work with them to solve their clinical problems.

You can give examples of when you **worked in a team** or **demonstrated leadership skills.**

It is a good idea to prepare your bullet points on paper before you practice. Do not be afraid to speak at some length but your points should be concise, complete and sincere. Be mindful not to waffle and make sure that you are engaging the interviewers. Your aim is to demonstrate that your desire to be a doctor is genuine, based on careful consideration and concordant with your skills and personality.

 'Why would you like to study at this medical school?'

A convincing answer to this question can go a long way to winning you a place. You should find out as much as you possibly can about the medical schools to which you have applied (ideally before applying to them!), and this means going beyond the prospectus! Try to visit the medical school and the surrounding area, meet and stay in touch with students and staff whom you meet, discuss any questions that you have on the online forums, and find out about the hospitals where clinical teaching takes place.

When answering this question, it is important to discuss the medical school's unique features. Giving more general responses that could apply to many other medical schools gives your answer less weight and originality.

There are a number of key areas that you can address:

- What you have learnt from speaking to students and staff from the medical school
- Any particular features of the course that appeal to you

- The facilities that are available on campus – especially academic facilities
- The appeal of the location – particularly from a health perspective
- Areas of research interest at the medical school
- The reputation of the hospitals where clinical attachments take place
- Personal reasons such as family commitments.

Example

I was initially drawn to Leeds because of the Leeds University Research Enterprise (LURE), which provides an excellent opportunity to undertake some early research. I then decided to visit the medical school at an open day and was shown around by some fourth-year students. We have kept in touch and what has impressed me the most is how much they refer to the approachability of the staff, and how they are made to feel like one of the team by the doctors on their clinical placements. I have found Leeds to be a vibrant, multicultural city that offers exposure to the different health problems experienced by the various communities. I am also aware that "Jimmy's" and the Leeds General Infirmary are two internationally renowned teaching hospitals, which provide an excellent clinical experience for students and carry out lots of world-class research in areas such as cancer.'

 Questions relating to your experiences, achievements and personal qualities.

The interviewers are likely to ask you questions relating to the experiences that you have introduced in your personal statement or in relation to the desirable qualities of a good doctor (see Chapter 6).

For these types of questions, consider using the **SPAR** approach:

Situation OR
Problem
Action
Result/Reflection/Relevance to being a doctor

Examples

	A 'Tell us about your work experience.'	**B** 'Can you think of a time where you demonstrated leadership skills?'
Situation or problem	*This should be a short statement setting the scene:*	
	'I undertook 2 weeks of work experience at Queen's Hospital with the neurosurgical team.'	'During one of our Duke of Edinburgh expeditions, we had ended up in the wrong place and were short on time.'
Action	*What you did – where possible, you need to make your personal skills come through. Make use of 'power' verbs!*	
	'I accompanied the junior doctors in their daily work, including ward rounds and multidisciplinary team meetings. I was also able to have excellent experiences with the consultant in theatre and in his clinics. In the clinics, I appreciated the importance of good communication skills when speaking to patients and their families, especially when breaking bad news. In theatre, I was fascinated by the synchronized roles being performed by the various members of staff, the skill and concentration of the surgeon, and the state-of-the-art equipment being used.'	'Despite being physically and mentally exhausted, I realized that we needed to make up ground if we were to make it to the campsite. I pulled everyone together for a meeting and told them we were going to be positive and move on from our mistakes. I made sure that everyone was happy with the route we were going to take and led from the front, keeping a fast pace and regularly dropping back to offer encouragement. We ended up making it to the campsite in excellent time and were in good spirits for the next day.'
Result/reflection/ relevance to being a doctor	*Conclude your answers by referring to what you have learnt and why it is relevant to being a doctor*	
	'Despite the challenges that the doctors faced every day, the experience motivated me further to become one myself in the future. I enjoyed working in a busy environment based on interaction with both patients and colleagues. I have also developed an early interest in neurosurgery.'	'I anticipate that, as a doctor, there will be times when, as a team, we make the wrong decisions. Left unaddressed, this can lead to low morale, which can have negative consequences on patient care. It is therefore important to show leadership and initiative by listening to and motivating colleagues.'

If you are asked a more general question regarding the personal qualities of doctors, a different approach is required. Begin by listing the relevant qualities in answer to the question, but you MUST conclude by introducing situations where you have demonstrated these qualities. There is a possibility that this will lead to more specific questions (see Example B, above) where you can elaborate using SPAR.

Example

What are the qualities of a good doctor?

1. Recognize the qualities of a good doctor (see Chapter 6).

2. Choose three that can be applied to yourself and elaborate why they are important in a doctor, for example:

   Good communication skills: to build the trust of your patients and to be able to explain any advice that you have in an accessible way.

   Team working skills: it is important to collaborate with other doctors and health-care professionals in order to meet each patient's individual needs.

   Spirit of enquiry: doctors should make a point of attending conferences and reading relevant journals to ensure that their practice is up to date.

3. Extend your answer to demonstrate how you possess these qualities:

   Good communications skills: 'During my voluntary work at the local hospital, I spent time speaking to patients who were being treated for cancer. I learnt how important it is to empathize with patients and listen to their concerns and expectations in order to build a rapport with them.'

   Team working skills: 'As a member of the school basketball team, I am aware of the importance of being a team player both on and off the court. On the court, I ensure that I concentrate on fulfilling my role and that I maintain constant communication with my team mates to address any ideas or problems. Off the court, I help ensure that morale is up, even if we lose, and provide and receive constructive criticism so that we can move forward together. I also try to be flexible if other team mates want to reschedule training.'

> **Spirit of enquiry:** 'I make an effort to read some interesting articles from *The Lancet* in my school library, which allows me to remain aware of important contemporary health issues such malaria. I also use the Internet to find out more about various issues.'

'What are your weaknesses?'

This is one of the toughest questions asked by interviewers (although it is a very easy question to ask!). Candidates need to strike the balance of not painting themselves in a negative light, while demonstrating an insight into their shortcomings. One approach to this dilemma is to present 'positive' weaknesses, such as:

- Becoming emotionally attached to patients
- Burdening yourself with too many commitments
- For science graduates: clinical medicine is based on approximations rather than scientific precision, and so you will need to adapt to this way of thinking.

As with questions concerning your strengths, it is important to liven up your answer with a specific example and an explanation of the steps that you are taking to tackle these weaknesses.

Example

'I currently work as a volunteer on an oncology ward and, while doing this, I have got to know a number of the patients. Recently, one of the patients, a young man whom I spoke to regularly, died. I was deeply saddened by this and, for the next few days, I was unable to concentrate on my studies. I sought advice from one of the nurses from the ward, who told me it was a natural reaction because of my inexperience and that it is important to put those thoughts to one side and not let it affect my academic performance. Since then, I have recognized that death is a feature of hospital medicine and that it should serve as a motivation for me to do the best that I can at all times.'

'Why have you not decided to become a nurse?'

The reason that interviewers ask this question is to assess:

1. How well you understand the role of doctors and nurses (or other health-care professionals)
2. Whether or not you respect the work of other health-care professionals.

It is therefore important to have a good understanding of the great differences within the professions and to acknowledge the indispensable role that nurses play:

- Nursing is a very diverse profession in itself and nurses are trained for many of the technical aspects of patient care – from administering drugs on the hospital ward, to changing dressings for patients at their homes and assisting surgeons in theatre.
- Doctors are ultimately responsible for patients and are required to diagnose and formulate management plans for each. Their job involves more problem-solving and the application of both broader and deeper scientific knowledge. Some senior specialist nurses now also have similar responsibilities but most do not. Nurses and other health-care professionals work alongside doctors to provide the optimal care and it is important that there is communication between all parties to ensure this.
- Doctors are able to undertake medical research, which can improve the diagnostic and therapeutic options for patients. Nursing research is related more to improving nursing practices.

Political, historical and ethical questions

Examples include:

- 'What do you think of all the changes to job application processes for junior doctors?'

- 'What is the greatest medical development in the last century?'
- 'What is wrong with the NHS?'
- 'Should euthanasia be legalized?
- 'What do you think about the use of animals in drug testing?'

The purpose of such questions is to assess your interests and awareness and whether you have an opinion or ideas about current medical affairs (see Chapter 11 for more information on issues about which you may be expected to know).

The most important aspect when answering these questions is to show awareness of the different aspects of the argument before concluding with your own opinion on the subject. Structure your answer as follows:

- Introduction – briefly outline the status quo
- Arguments for
- Arguments against
- Additional factors to consider
- Conclusion with a balanced opinion.

If you are asked questions on the NHS, your answer can referenced to either something that you saw on work experience or that you have read, and it is important to mention this in your answer.

Example

Should euthanasia be legalized?

Introduction

This is a very important and pertinent ethical issue with compelling arguments on both sides. I am aware that, at the moment, in the UK, patients have the autonomy to refuse life-saving treatment provided that they are competent, but it is illegal for anyone to perform euthanasia or assist suicide. However, euthanasia is legal in countries such as the Netherlands and Belgium, and, in Switzerland, it is legal to assist suicide.

For

On the one hand, doctors are expected to act according to their patients' wishes and it is conceivable that, for some patients with chronic diseases, they would prefer to die a peaceful and dignified death than continue to live in suffering.

Against

On the other hand, doctors are bound by the principle of non-maleficence, that is to 'first, do no harm' and there can be no greater harm than killing. Another issue is that medical research is always evolving and there is a possibility that treatment for a chronic disease can drastically improve. Similarly, prognostic indicators are not always correct and some patients do better than expected. There is also a slippery slope, as patients may make impulsive decisions to end their lives from which there is no turning back.

Other issues

It is important, and often forgotten, that this issue should not be discussed in isolation and we should look further at why someone would want to end their life in the first place. There may be issues such as patients feeling that they are a burden on their families both emotionally and financially, or some may feel isolated because their families are not in a position to look after them and they live in care homes. Perhaps the government should consider providing more carers to help look after patients at home or provide improved benefits for family members who look after their loved ones.

Conclusion

In my opinion, patients should have the freedom to choose to end their lives as long as a panel of doctors agree that this is a reasonable request, made free from coercion. Doctors should also have the right to refuse to perform euthanasia and be able to refer the patient to a colleague. However, this should happen only if committed steps are taken to improve the social care of patients when they are at home so that, despite suffering from chronic diseases, they and their families are eased of external stressors that can make living even more painful.

Questions on what you have read

Candidates are sometimes asked if they have read any interesting journal articles or books recently.

Try to get a hold of one or two recent articles that interest you and that you are able to understand from a high-impact medical journal such as *Nature Medicine* or *The Lancet*. Write down a brief summary of the article in a few bullet points which will convey the findings and the message of the article to the interviewer. You can also consider the importance and the relevance of the article in the broader context of everyday medical practice.

Similarly, be prepared to summarize a book that you have read and express your opinion on it. It is not important whether you choose fiction or non-fiction, as long as you are capable of providing a summary and are able to give an opinion on it. You can also provide further details of how much you read or of your other hobbies.

Asking a question at the end

At the end of the interview, it is likely that the interviewers will invite you to ask them a question. You can always decline this offer and tell them that students and staff have already answered everything that you wanted to know. However, if you do choose to ask something, make sure that it is not something that can be easily discovered on the medical school website or prospectus, as this may indicate lack of research on your part. Something along the lines of 'Are there going to be any changes to the curriculum next year?' addresses a genuine issue for a prospective student and shows a keen interest in studies.

On the day

Look the part

Remember that some people still hold prejudices based on appearance, so it is better to be safe than sorry! Go for smart and professional but comfortable dress unless the university has specified otherwise on the invitation. Do not forget simple things such as tidy hair and polished shoes. Men should wear a dark suit with a tie and remember dark socks and a done-up collar; if you sport a beard, keep it neat. Women can also go for a suit, although a blouse with a skirt at least knee length or pair of trousers is perfectly acceptable – avoid visible cleavage and bare midriffs!

Get there early

The interview is stressful enough without having to worry about getting there on time! Arriving early also provides an opportunity to feel at home and absorb the vibes of the campus surroundings. Have a drink of water to keep your throat clear.

Be friendly

The waiting room will be full of other candidates who are either waiting or have just finished. Most of them will be friendly, and engaging in conversation will allow you to relax without losing your focus. Some schools have admitted to watching the interaction between candidates in the waiting room, so it is a chance to apply your communication skills – be neither shy nor overbearing, listen keenly to what everyone has to say and warmly wish others the best as they are called in. Eventually, you will be called in and taken to your interview.

Oxbridge interviews

Interviews at Oxford and Cambridge have traditionally been very different from those at the other medical schools. Each college runs its own interviews and often over two separate sessions – one covering the more conventional areas addressed above, the other to ensure that you are academically capable. In the academic interview, you will be tested on your logic and reasoning skills, as well as your ability to think quickly. It is a good idea to prepare for this by brushing up on your science and maths, as well as practising some challenging problems. You might also be invited to interviews at another college as an alternative to your first choice.

Most Oxbridge invitations will ask you to dress comfortably and there will be no need for suits. However, be presentable if casual in your appearance and don't let any flamboyant choices in attire distract the interviewers!

11 Hot topics in medicine

With Veena Naganathar, Asil Tahir, Pairaw Kader and Omar Chehab

In interviews, medical schools often test applicants on their understanding of medical current affairs. A genuine appreciation comes through strongly and will endear you to the panel! Although it requires effort to read and discuss topical issues, this does not need to be a chore. We encourage working in groups (see Chapter 5) and using varied media such as the internet, journals, books and films to gain an understanding and get your thought processes moving on issues that are not necessarily academic.

Keeping abreast of the news

The Internet has profoundly enhanced our accessibility to information and there is a lot to be discovered! Keep up to date with daily news on news websites and television broadcasts – every day there are issues related to health problems in the UK and around the world. At all times, you should remember to remain critical of what you read and to place it in the context of *who* the story is trying to address and *what* message it is trying to convey.

Medicine in literature and film

Books and films are a great source of inspiration and entertainment and there are many available. Some bring to life the experiences and discoveries of fascinating individuals, while others can spark debate on ethical dilemas and contentious issues. Below we've listed some of the books and films that we have enjoyed. Try to read or watch a few – we hope that they will get your thoughts flowing, as well as keep you entertained.

Books

Burton N. *The Meaning of Madness*. Oxford: Achean Press, 2008.
An exploration of mental illnesses and how it is associated with normal human behaviour.

Fadiman A. *The Spirit Catches You and You Fall Down: A Hmong Child, Her American Doctors, the Collision of Two Cultures*. New York: Farrar, Straus and Giroux, 1998.
This award-winning, compelling read about an epileptic child and her family powerfully demonstrates the importance of cultural awareness in medical practice.

Gawande A. *Better: A Surgeon's Notes on Performance*. London: Profile Books Ltd, 2007.
A well-written account of the virtues required to be a successful doctor.

Gawande A. *Complications: A Surgeon's Notes on an Imperfect Science*. London: Profile Books Ltd, 2002.
A book that humanizes doctors and discusses the important role of human error in practice.

Kesey K. *One Flew Over the Cuckoo's Nest*. London: Penguin, 1962.
A free-spirited man pays the price for challenging the oppressive paternalism of a psychiatric asylum. This became an Oscar-winning film starring Jack Nicholson.

Pemberton M. *Trust Me I'm A Junior Doctor*. London: Hodder, 2008.
A funny and honest account of the experiences of a house officer in the UK.

Pisani E. *The Wisdom of Whores: Bureaucrats, Brothels and the Business of AIDS*. London: Granta Books, 2008.
Everything that you need to know about the HIV/AIDS pandemic as well as a critique of the political, social and economic obstacles to solving it.

Pollock AM. *NHS PLC: The Privatisation of Our Health Care*. London: Verso, 2004.
A revealing guide to health politics in the UK.

Porter R. *The Greatest Benefit to Mankind*. London: Harper Collins Ltd, 1999.
An engaging and comprehensive tour through the history of medicine.

Ramachandran M and Ronson M. *The Medical Miscellany*. London: Hammersmith Press Ltd, 2005.
A fascinating collection of medically related items that will give you a perspective on medicine and health care not available from other books.

Rose S. *Lifelines*. London: Vintage, 2005.
An exploration of the importance of the complex interactions between organisms and their environment, dismissing the notion that everything about us can be explained through genes.

Thomas V. *Partners of The Heart: Vivien Thomas and his Work with Alfred Blalock*. Philadelphia: University of Pennsylvania Press, 1986.
The little-known account of an African–American research technician who played a pioneering role in the birth of heart surgery against a backdrop of racial division in mid-twentieth century America.

Films

Awakenings (1990)

Starring Robin Williams and Robert De Niro. Based on a true story by Oliver Sacks, about a doctor's discovery of a 'cure' for sleeping sickness and the difficulties adjusting to normality for one of his patients.

John Q (2002)

Starring Denzel Washington. Based in the US, the story of a desperate father's attempt to find a life-saving heart transplant for his young son after he learns that it is not covered by insurance. In the hope of saving his son, he holds the hospital's emergency department hostage.

Miss Evers' Boys (1997)

Starring Alfre Woodard and Laurence Fishburne. The true story of the infamous Tuskegee study where the US public health service withheld treatment from African–American syphilis sufferers for decades to study the natural progression of the disease.

Patch Adams (1998)

Starring Robin Williams. The true story of a medical student who challenges conservative medical practice by introducing humour and compassion to the doctor–patient relationship.

Philadelphia (1993)

Starring Tom Hanks and Denzel Washington. Based on the true story of an American lawyer who was dismissed by his employers in one of the first AIDS discrimination cases. His personal injury attorney overcomes his own prejudices and ignorance to fight the case.

Sicko (2007)

Starring Michael Moore. Moore reveals the shortfalls of the American health-care system, and travels to Britain, Canada, France and Cuba to emphasize its failures.

Something the Lord Made (2004)

Starring Mos Def and Alan Rickman. A film adaptation of Partners of the Heart (see under Books).

Vera Drake (2004)

Starring Imelda Staunton. The story of a well-intentioned backstreet abortionist in 1950s' Britain whose life is thrown into turmoil when she is caught by the police.

Hot topics

In this section, we hope to motivate you to find out more about the medical world and that this motivation serves as an inspiration for a lifelong passion. We would emphasize that you should not memorize what is written here, but try to read it as if you were reading it for leisure to gain a basic understanding.

Professionalism

Duties of a doctor

The GMC (General Medical Council) has outlined the professional duties that doctors need to abide by in order to maintain their professional integrity:

- Make the care of your patient your first concern
- Protect and promote the health of patients and the public
- Provide a good standard of practice and care:
  - keep your professional knowledge and skills up to date
  - recognize and work within the limits of your competence
  - work with colleagues in the ways that best serve patients' interests
- Treat patients as individuals and respect their dignity:
  - treat patients politely and considerately
  - respect patients' right to confidentiality
- Work in partnership with patients:
  - listen to patients and respond to their concerns and preferences
  - give patients the information that they want or need in a way that they can understand
  - respect patients' rights to reach decisions with you about their treatment and care
  - support patients in caring for themselves to improve and maintain their health

- Be honest and open and act with integrity:
  - act without delay if you have good reason to believe that you or a colleague may be putting patients at risk
  - never discriminate unfairly against patients or colleagues
  - never abuse your patients' trust in you or the public's trust in the profession.

To read in greater detail about each duty, see: www.gmc-uk.org/ guidance/good_medical_practice/duties_of_a_doctor.asp

These can be applied to many interview situations from 'What do you think makes a good doctor?' to 'How do you think a doctor faced with problem X should deal with situation?'.

Working with others

Team work is an essential tool for patient care. Respecting and appreciating colleagues helps days run smoother and makes life easier. From time to time, however, problems may arise. Regardless of what the problem may be, your priority must always be **patient safety**. If you are faced with a question relating to a scenario where team unity has been fractured, bear this in mind first and foremost.

Figure 11.1 can be used as a mind map for answering these questions.

Accepting gifts

Once you qualify, you may find yourself inundated with gifts from patients and company representatives. Although chocolates and wine may be easy to accept without a second thought, how about a holiday or a car? The GMC recommends that you should be open about all financial dealings, which might include gifts of high value. What are the patients' motivations, what do they want in return and what will it mean to you? There should be no strings attached to the gifts. All details should be openly discussed and laid out on the table.

Pharmaceutical companies offer gifts and paid trips to conferences in the hope of swaying prescription in their favour. The extent of your obligations will depend on the value of the gift, so you must always be wary. Are the contents of the conference in Fiji of explicit benefit to your clinical practice? You should always emphasize the importance of being aware of the risks and not falling into any traps.

Your **probity** as a doctor should be of primary concern and should not be sabotaged for financial gain. Some institutions have regulations regarding gifts, with registers for gifts over a certain value. If there are any unresolved ethical concerns over the gifts, you can always seek advice from medical defence organizations

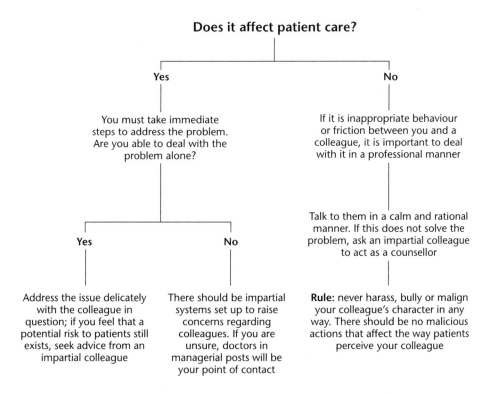

Figure 11.1 A mind map for tackling professional conflict.

such as the Medical Defence Union (MDU) or Medical Protection Society (MPS).

The NHS

The NHS is quite a common area of discussion in interviews, especially with the current financial and political climate, and the difficulties faced in maintaining the needs of the public.

Due to constant change, the issues that surround the NHS are important not only for your interview but also for you as a future employee.

Brief history

The NHS was introduced in 1948 by Aneurin Bevan, the socialist health minister at the time. It was formed in the aftermath of World War II, on the principle that everyone in Britain 'from the cradle to the grave' should have health care regardless of wealth or status. The services were free at the point of access, financed from central taxation and available to all, even temporary residents and visitors from other countries. This is known as the 'welfare state'.

Current state

Since then, the population has increased as well as life expectancy. This has caused additional burden on the NHS due to a lack of corresponding increases in government spending. Recent successive governments have tried to tackle this through measures such as the introduction of the National Institute for Health and Clinical Excellence (NICE), private finance initiatives (PFI) and 'marketization'. NICE aims to ensure that the services provided by the NHS are cost-effective and up to date. PFI is the subcontracting of NHS areas to private companies, so that the NHS pays for the services provided by private companies. 'Marketization' is the creation of competitive forces, such that, NHS trusts need to meet targets and compete with each other and private providers in order to be financially rewarded.

Structure of the NHS (Figure 11.2)

Members of Parliament pass reforms based on their perception of the problems of the NHS and the needs of the population. These are then turned into targets or guidance by the Department of Health and distributed to the health authorities. The strategic health authorities (SHAs) plan the health care for the regions, which are then provided by the primary care trusts (PCTs) and the secondary health-care trusts. PCTs provide community services such as GPs, dentists, district nurses and pharmacies. Secondary health-care trusts provide hospital-based specialist services. Special health authorities are in charge of national health initiatives such as NICE and the National Blood Service.

Since its birth, the NHS has been through several reforms. Some of the most recent ones have had the greatest impact. The major changes brought in have been outlined below:

- NHS as a competitive market, with SHAs and PCTs acting as buyers from the secondary health-care trusts, which provide these services at a competitive rate.
- Computerization of the NHS, to reduce paperwork costs and improve efficiency.
- The introduction of NICE, to increase the effective spending and assess the use of new technologies and their implementation, such as anti-cancer drugs and in vitro fertilization (IVF) treatment.

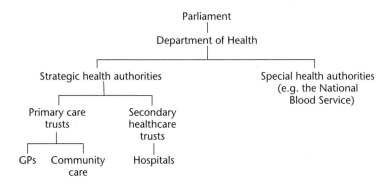

Figure 11.2 Structure of the NHS.

- Foundation trusts, which are hospitals that appoint their own board of trustees from the local population, who in turn decide how the hospitals within the trust should be run in order to optimize services and profits for the local population.
- Increase in patient choice with the 'Choose and Book' system, where patients can decide which hospital they want to be treated in for non-emergency procedures.
- New funding system known as tariffs, where NHS and private hospitals are paid per patient treated.

The public–private interface

In the UK, private health-care providers run alongside the NHS. Consultants can choose to work in private practice in addition to their NHS contractual hours. The number of hours that they can dedicate to private work depends on their contract. The Department of Health states that private work should never impinge on the NHS and the consultants' NHS obligations should always take priority.

Since the newer reforms, NHS and private systems are becoming increasingly integrated, with NHS buildings and machinery, such as scanners for magnetic resonance imaging (MRI), being rented out to private providers. As the restructuring encourages private practices to compete against NHS services for patients, there have been conflicts of interests with NHS consultants who work in private practices. Are they to act in the best interest of the NHS or the best interest of their private practice? To deal with this predicament, the Department of Health set out guidelines for consultants who partake in private practice:

- NHS organizations and consultants should work together to ensure there is no conflict of interest between private practice and NHS work.
- Private work should not disadvantage NHS patients or services.
- NHS commitments should take precedence unless it is to provide emergency care.
- NHS facilities can be used only with prior consent from the NHS employers.

- Doctors who do private work should not be discriminated against.

www.nhsemployers.org/SiteCollectionDocuments/code_of_
conduct_for_private_practice_190208_aw.pdf

The arguments for and against private health care

In an interview, you may be asked to comment on this issue, for which you will need to present both sides of the argument and then give a clear and logical opinion. Remember that members of the panel may have private commitments or may be opposed to private practice, so it is important to represent all sides of the argument and deliver your answer politely. As long as your opinion is well structured and justified, it should be acceptable to all.

Arguments for

- If an individual can afford private health care, they should have the freedom and right to choose.
- Private practices use NHS facilities, thus bring money into the NHS.
- Patients who use private health care still pay the mandatory National Insurance contributions and so are not taking funds away from the NHS. This money can be used for those who cannot afford to contribute to the central funds.
- Doctors who want to supplement their earnings in their spare time should have the freedom to do so.
- Taking away private health care may reduce the number of doctors, as medicine in the UK would become a less attractive career financially.
- The private sector eases the burden on the NHS.

Arguments against

- There is a two-tier system, with only those able to afford private care having the choice of using it.
- The private patients who are referred to NHS facilities may jump the queue. In addition, those using NHS facilities in an

emergency may use the time of NHS staff. Both of these could mean that NHS patients are disadvantaged.

- Centrally and publicly funded NHS facilities should exclusively be used for NHS patients.
- Money put into private health care can be redirected to the NHS through increasing taxes for those with a disposable income.
- Increasing health workers' pay would mean that they would not seek private work, because they would be satisfied with their NHS income.
- Private practices cannot afford to provide all services and so, in an emergency situation, patients may need to be transferred to an NHS hospital, losing valuable time and perhaps being detrimental to their care.
- When care is money-driven, the doctor becomes a business-person, acting to please the 'customer' and to increase profits.
- Advertising and negative media can persuade people who cannot afford private care to buy private policies.

The limits of the NHS

Should the NHS provide non-essential health services, such as alternative or complementary therapies or cosmetic surgery? Again, we need to look at the pros and cons of the subject and give a balanced argument.

Alternative or complementary therapies are unconventional treatments, including homoeopathy, acupuncture, aromatherapy, hypnosis and Chinese herbal medicine. They are taken instead of (alternative) or alongside (complementary) conventional treatment.

The advantages of these therapies

- They provide a lot of one-on-one contact, which may prove beneficial to the patient in a psychological and spiritual manner, providing holistic care.
- They may offer hope to patients where conventional treatment has failed.
- Many complementary therapies are not invasive and non-toxic, so do little harm.

- It would be better have these therapies regulated by the NHS, to help ensure patient safety and reduce the risk of vulnerable patients being exploited.

The disadvantages

- These therapies are not evidence-based, with results being anecdotal or not reproducible.
- It is a poorly regulated field, with some therapies being known to be harmful:
  - in Chinese herbal medicine, toxic substances such as steroids and amphetamines are sold as part of 'herbal' concoctions
  - some alternative substances are toxic (for example, St John's wort for depression can cause liver toxicity) and can interact with conventional treatment.
- Therapists are not medically trained and may not be knowledgeable about conventional treatment, which may lead to misinformation.
- They are generally expensive.

With better research into the mechanisms of action, side effects and interactions, as well as strict regulations on production, prescription and training, clinical judgement can be made in a more evidence-based manner. At the moment, due to the lack of evidence and safety concerns, it may not be safe to freely promote the use of all alternative and complementary therapies.

Cosmetic surgery is a subjective term. For a seemingly good-looking woman, who wants a rhinoplasty (nose job), her image of her nose may lead to depression. For an athletic young man with severe myopia and intolerance to contact lenses, laser vision correction may enable him to become a competitive athlete and fulfil his life ambitions. Are these non-essential?

For funding these treatments

- A procedure that may seem medically unnecessary may improve psychological well-being and save spending on the provision of mental health care through counselling and medical treatment of depression.

- If not provided by the NHS, poor patients may seek these treatments from expensive providers, leading to debt.

Against funding

- Cosmetic surgery may be a sign of issues with body image, which may suggest deeper issues of self-esteem or depression. These issues may be better treated through counselling and treatment of the underlying problem.
- It is unfair to spend public funds on cosmetic surgery, which may be due to only one person's perception of what is wrong.
- As it would in effect be 'free', there may be excessive demands for cosmetic surgery.

Primary care

Primary care encompasses all community-based health services, including GPs, community and practice nurses, community therapists (e.g. physiotherapists and speech and language therapists), pharmacists, optometrists, dentists and midwives. These are the first and sometimes the only point of contact to the health services for the public. These services are provided by PCTs.

Much of the reforms and modernization of the NHS has been centred on PCTs. They are responsible for assessing and providing for the local health-care needs by:

- implementing community health-care programmes, such as smoking cessation, health screening and physical fitness programmes
- integrating health care provided by the NHS with social care provided by local authorities, social services and voluntary organizations
- ensuring that buildings, equipment and staff are constantly updated to provide these services for the community.

Under the new reforms, the PCTs, who hold 80% of the health-care budget, have been given more direct control over the commissioning of services. It is hoped that this will guarantee efficient delivery of services tailored to the local population.

In a recent review of the NHS by Lord Ara Darzi, many of the changes that he recommended were in primary care. With emphasis on improving quality of care by having 'polyclinics' that provide services in the local vicinity, local district general hospitals (DGHs), which are thought to be an inefficient source of spending, can be closed or downgraded. This means less local access to services such as accident and emergency and imaging services. The PCTs may have to commission these services from other hospitals, polyclinics or private companies to provide for their community.

There have been fears that the heavy integration of private services and dismantling of the local hospitals in preference for 'quality' of specialist care provided may reduce the access and availability of care for the public, with possible introductions of fees for certain services. There are also concerns that the continuity of care provided by the GP may be fractured because patients will increasingly find specialists as the first port of call in polyclinics, where a holistic approach may be compromised.

www.ournhs.nhs.uk
www.healthemergency.org.uk/pdf/Darziresponsecriticalgaps.pdf

The multidisciplinary team and holistic care

A multidisciplinary team (MDT) is made up of professionals from several different backgrounds, such as doctors from different specialties, nurses, physiotherapists, speech and language therapists, dieticians, and social workers. This enables the care of the patient to be coordinated and well managed. MDTs have been especially successful in complicated diseases such as cancer, stroke and mental illness, where patients may have not only physical symptoms, but also psychological and social problems.

Take, for example, a case of laryngeal cancer discussed in an MDT meeting:

- The radiologist looks at the scans to assess the location of the cancer and where it may have spread to.
- The histopathologist gives an opinion on the tissue sample taken as to the type of cancer it is.

- From this, the head and neck surgeon and the oncologists are able to formulate a treatment plan, be it surgery, chemotherapy or radiotherapy.
- The speech and language therapist and dietician give their opinion on how to improve the patient's ability to talk or eat if this has been affected by either the disease or the side effects of treatment.
- The specialist oncology (Macmillan) nurse follows the patient up regularly and delves deeply into social and psychological concerns for them and their families.
- This information is constantly fed back to the GP, who has closer contact with the patient, provides constant feedback, follows the patient up regularly and keeps an eye out for recurring symptoms.

Actions that may have taken weeks to execute through letters and phone calls can be discussed all at once in an MDT meeting and these different professionals can all carry out their duties to the patient simultaneously, ensuring prompt care. A good MDT meeting enables not only smooth execution of patient care but also better understanding and appreciation of each other's professions, which can help doctors know what help they can call upon.

Holistic medicine is exactly this – treating the patient and not just the disease. A severe illness such as this has detrimental effects on a person's life, which may be irreversible even if the disease is cured. The psychological shock from the recent diagnosis of a possibly life-threatening illness, the social difficulties from the stress that it may have caused the family and financial difficulties from having to give up days of work to stay in hospital reduce the patient's quality of life even further.

Nosocomial infections

Nosocomial (derived from the Greek word for hospital: *nosokomeion*) infections or hospital-acquired infections are infectious diseases secondary to the patient's initial problem that manifest from 48 hours of admission to 30 days after discharge.

The most common nosocomial infections are urinary tract infections, pneumonias and wound site infections.

 Around 7.8% of patients in the UK present with a nosocomial infection, which increases their stay in hospital by 2.5 times on average. This is estimated to cost the NHS £1 billion

Severe illnesses cause people to become immunocompromised, making it easier for them to contract infections. Patients who have had invasive procedures such as venepuncture, cannulation and surgery have had their natural protective barriers infiltrated, making it easier for microorganisms to invade. The movement of staff and equipment from one patient to another, as well as crowded open wards, makes cross-infection much easier.

Cross-infections have become more common recently due to:

- patients resident in hospitals being generally more ill, and therefore more immunocompromised, as a result of improvements in outpatient and primary care
- an increase in older patients, who are more immuno-compromised
- greater use of immunosuppressant drugs
- careless prescription of antibiotics, leading to resistance.

The spread of these infections can be prevented by:

- improvement in ward cleaning
- washing/sterilizing hands between patients
- barrier nursing of patients known to have infectious diseases, using side rooms, aprons, gloves and masks if necessary
- protocols for antibiotic prescription.

www.eurosurveillance.org/ViewArticle.aspx?ArticleId=4

Clinical governance

Clinical governance is a framework to maintain high standards of care through continuous assessment and improvement of services provided by the NHS. This is a rather complicated concept and is something that most medical students know very little about.

You will not be expected to give an elaborate answer on this topic, but a basic appreciation will be impressive. Some aspects, such as 'evidence-based medicine' and 'continuous professional development', are important and need to be well understood.

Clinical governance is made up of seven elements (Figure 11.3):

1. **Clinical effectiveness**: this ensures that health care is up to date and the needs are met as outlined by the National Service Framework (NSF).
2. **Research and development**: all clinical practices and treatment should be based on evidence from studies to show their effectiveness (evidence-based medicine) and there should be constant efforts to improve, especially in areas that have a huge burden on society, such as cardiovascular diseases and cancer.

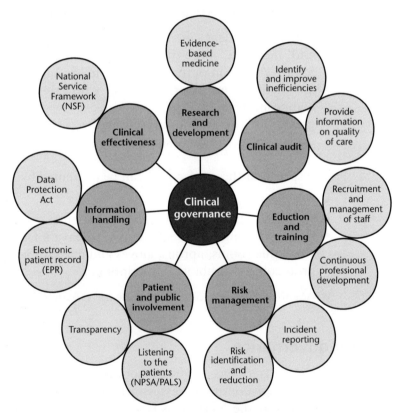

Figure 11.3 The elements of clinical governance. NPSA, National Patient Safety Agency; PALS, Patient Advice and Liaison Services.

3. **Clinical audit**: this is a systematic review of services to ensure that the highest quality care and treatment are provided to patients. It consists of initially identifying weaknesses in practice, establishing the correct standard of care, implementing changes to improve, and then reassessing the practice to see if the improvements have improved quality and are being sustained.

4. **Education and training**: as with treatment, the staff also need to be of the highest quality. This is determined by the recruitment, management and training of the staff. An important aspect of medicine is 'continuous professional development', where all NHS professionals are responsible for improving their knowledge and being up to date with the latest developments in practice. Their knowledge and development are assessed annually by appraisals conducted by their seniors and colleagues.

5. **Risk management**: this involves identifying possible risks to patients and staff, and taking measures to avoid them. These can include errors in patient treatment, violence towards staff and patients, nosocomial infections, and minor accidents on premises. Incident reporting also encourages openness about errors so that staff can admit to mistakes for everyone to learn from.

6. **Patient and public involvement**: this aspect is to encourage good communication between the public and the profession about their needs. Transparency about complaints procedures and errors made by doctors and hospitals enhances patient safety. Organizations such as The National Patient Safety Agency (NPSA) and Patient Advice and Liaison Services (PALS) play an important role in this.

7. **Information handling**: the NHS needs to give health-care professionals straightforward but controlled access to information on patients. This can facilitate complaints procedures, audits, clinical effectiveness and risk management. This has been improved by the NHS Care Records Service (CRS). Patient information is protected by the Data Protection Act and the Confidentiality Act.

European Working Time Directive

From 1 August 2009, the European Working Time Directive (EWTD) was implemented in the NHS, with all doctors restricted to 48 hours of work in a week, with a maximum of 13 hours in any 24-hour period.

There are pros and cons as shown in Table 11.1.

Table 11.1 Pros and cons of the European Working Time Directive

Pros	Cons
Better work–life balance	Reduced patient contact and reduced opportunities for hands-on training
Safer for patients as most non-emergency cases are dealt with during daytime hours	Lower wages
Increased places at medical school	More risk of miscommunication as several doctors may see an individual patient during their stay
Increasing role of nurses may improve continuity of care, nurses' pay and professional satisfaction and may prove more cost-effective	Increased cost in training doctors
	Extending the role of nurses may be very protocol-based and therefore limited. It may also take valuable training away from junior doctors and what used to be a junior doctor's job may be carried out by nurses

Global health

Global health covers issues that are a burden on the world as a whole and not just a small region or a nation. The diseases of main global concern currently include HIV/AIDS, malaria, diarrhoeal illnesses, nutritional deficiency, tuberculosis and obesity. There are several precipitants for global health issues, most notably financial and political inequality.

As an example, diarrhoeal diseases are a group of diseases that are relatively easily preventable by straightforward measures such as improved sanitation with basic sewage and water systems combined with immunizations. However, due to several factors, including, the lack of interest by global corporations such as pharmaceutical companies and mounting debts in developing countries, these measures are not always applied. This is an example of health inequality on a global scale.

Medical ethics

We all have a personal opinion as to what we may feel is morally right in a specific situation. Many of the ethical cases raised in medical interviews have no clear right or wrong answers. Instead, the interviewers will mainly be assessing whether you approach ethical dilemmas in a rational manner by having an appreciation of different perspectives. Valid reasoning is important to put forward a logically sound argument based on consistent principles. It is therefore useful to have a basic understanding of the important principles of medical ethics that doctors are expected to be guided by.

The four ethical principles of medicine

These principles can be used to justify different points of views to ethical dilemmas.

1. Autonomy

This is the capacity to think, decide, and act freely and independently. A patient's autonomy must be respected and they are entitled to make non-coerced decisions for themselves. They have the right to choose whether to take or refuse treatment, and the doctor has a duty to provide them with all the information that they need in order to make an informed decision.

2. Beneficence

This word originates from the Latin *bene* meaning 'good' and *facere* meaning 'to do'. This principle emphasizes that doctors must act in the patient's and/or society's best interest. In most situations, the principle of beneficence and respecting a patient's autonomy go hand in hand. However, if there is a conflict where the patient's choice is not deemed by the doctors to be in their best interest, then the first principle of autonomy must be followed and the decision must ultimately be left to the patient.

3. Non-maleficence

The third principle derives from the Latin *male* meaning 'harmful'. Doctors must always 'do no harm' to patients. This can be seen as a similar principle to that of beneficence, because doing no harm corresponds to doing what is best for the patient. The main reason for having this principle is to have a baseline duty to all patients.

4. Justice

As resources and time are finite, doctors are commonly put in situations where they will need to consider limiting treatment or time spent on some patients. The principle of justice is involved in the fair distribution of resources across the population, including money, time and organs. Patients in similar positions should be treated equally and should have access to health care on the basis of their clinical needs without discrimination.

Informed consent

Informed consent is based on the principle of patient autonomy. A competent patient has the right to refuse any examination, investigation or treatment after being fully informed of all the facts required to make such a decision. The patient, however, does not have the right to demand treatment. Voluntary informed consent must be obtained without coercion from every competent patient before any clinical, scientific (research) or other intervention is given. For this to take place, patients must be fully informed and made aware of:

- alternative options for treatment, including no treatment
- the aims of treatment with a clear medical plan
- possible benefits and risks with and without treatment
- possibility of changing their mind at any time and seeking a second opinion
- any other information that the patient requests.

Competence

Consent can be obtained only from patients who are competent. This means that patients have the capability to understand the information and retain it, as well as the ability to communicate and make an independent rational decision in response.

Most adults are assumed competent unless proven otherwise, such as having a mental disorder that prevents them from making a decision. If a patient is incompetent, no other adult can give consent on their behalf and the doctor must act in the patient's best interest. Relatives and friends can be a source of information to help determine a patient's best interest, but cannot give or withhold consent. Patients are able to issue advance directives, which are statements made by people when they are competent, stating how they would wish to be treated if they were to become incompetent in the future and incapable of making decisions on what is best for them. Using this, doctors would be able to respect the patient's autonomy even if it is deemed not to be in their best interests.

Children under the age of 16 years are presumed to be incompetent to consent unless they demonstrate a sufficient level of understanding and intelligence to make a decision. Children who are believed to have this capacity are considered 'Fraser-competent' (previously known as 'Gillick-competent') and can give consent for medical treatment. It is unlikely for children under the age of 13 to be considered Fraser-competent; although this is a grey area legally, any uncertainties should be cleared up in court. However, Fraser-competent children cannot refuse treatment if this is not deemed to be in their interest. If they do so, then consent for treatment must be obtained from those with parental responsibility or the matter must be taken to court.

Patient confidentiality

All doctors have a duty to protect the confidentiality of their patients and respect their autonomy. This is the cornerstone of the trust that is crucial to the patient–doctor relationship. If doctors are asked to provide information about a patient, it is important to seek that patient's consent for disclosure; ideally the information should be kept anonymous with minimal information revealed. Information on patients may be requested for many reasons, including education, research and administration.

Confidentiality may be broken in certain situations: if it is in society's interest or to protect the patient, or if the benefits of disclosure outweigh the benefits of maintaining confidentiality. The following are examples of when the duty of confidentiality can be relaxed:

- Notification of authorities for infectious outbreaks (e.g. meningitis, tuberculosis and measles)
- Suspected child abuse (this includes neglect and physical, sexual or emotional abuse)
- Informing the DVLA if a patient's condition may affect their driving (e.g. epilepsy or impaired vision)
- To assist in the prevention or detection of a serious crime.

HIV/AIDS

Human immunodeficiency virus (HIV)/acquired immune deficiency syndrome (AIDS) is a disease that was first reported in the 1980s and has reached pandemic proportions throughout the world.

HIV infects human hosts and, in order to survive, it attacks, evolves and spreads, killing immune cells (such as $CD4^+$ T-lymphocytes), which form our defence systems against bacteria and other microorganisms. If left untreated, the virus continues to spread rapidly and increases immunodeficiency. This leads to vulnerability to a number of microorganisms, which would otherwise not have had the capabilities to harm us, known as opportunistic infections.

AIDS is a term that is often used interchangeably with HIV; however, the two are not the same. AIDS is caused by HIV, but an individual only has AIDS once the $CD4^+$ cell count reaches a critically low level. At this stage, the alarmingly low number of white blood cells means that the infected person is vulnerable to a wide range of microorganisms that have the capability to cause a broad spectrum of diseases across the various organs in the body.

Transmission of HIV and preventive measures

It is clear to see that HIV is a serious condition that warrants urgent intervention. This starts with preventing infection in the first place. Before considering these measures, we must first consider the means by which this virus spreads from one person to the next:

1. Sexual intercourse
2. Via blood products
3. Transmission from mother to child during birth.

The risk of transmission by sex between an individual who has HIV to a person who doesn't varies from 0.04% to 1.7% per unprotected sexual act, depending on the route of entry. Consider the scenario that a person becomes infected with HIV by having sexual intercourse with a person who has HIV. If that person then has sexual contact with another person who is uninfected, he or she may then spread the disease further. Continuation of this cycle leads to an exponential growth in the number of people infected with HIV and eventually leads to an epidemic. This is in fact what happened with HIV before the discovery of the virus in 1981. The effects of this epidemic are still felt today, such that it is estimated that about 0.6% of the world's population is infected with HIV and, to date, AIDS has killed more than 25 million people.

The spread of HIV via blood products is a particular problem in intravenous drug users who share needles to administer recreational drugs. In doing so, the virus is passed from one person to another. This is why HIV has higher rates in recreational drug users. It is important to identify drug users so that they can be advised of the risks, which is no easy task, because people do not readily disclose their drug habits. It requires the development of a strong doctor–patient relationship based on trust, honesty and professionalism. It remains important to promote safe and responsible drug use, advocating the use of clean needles and safe injection sites, which are clean and away from areas that may lead to serious infections, such as the neck. Some local authorities have needle exchange programmes to promote the use of clean needles and healthier lifestyles.

The final route by which HIV can be transmitted is from mother to child during labour, commonly referred to as vertical transmission. This method of viral spread is, however, becoming less common in developed countries as a result of specialized care. Mothers with HIV who are pregnant are given antiretroviral drugs (see below) during their pregnancy and advised to avoid breast-feeding their babies. However, this is not the case in developing countries, where access to drugs and education is less widely available.

Treatment of HIV

The treatment of HIV requires the input of various health-care professionals from different specialties. The treatment primarily involves a triple therapy of antiretrovirals which are designed to target specific structural components of the virus. These drugs suppress the activity of the virus and prevent it from spreading and infecting new cells. In doing so, they help to maintain immunity in HIV-infected people. Although the drugs are effective at suppressing viral replication for a time period, they are by no means ideal and present many challenges to doctors prescribing them. Patients on antiretroviral therapy are required to adhere strictly to a demanding daily regimen, which involves taking several drugs at specific times. They are not a cure for HIV and infected individuals continue to harbour the virus in their system. With time, the virus will eventually continue to replicate and cause disease in its host.

Furthermore, these drugs have powerful effects on the body and in doing so often cause numerous side effects. This in turn can cause patients on HIV drugs to lose motivation and stop therapy. It is here that a doctor must use all her or his expertise to try to deter this from happening by taking a holistic approach. Doctors should try to be aware of any emotional issues that may be lingering subconsciously and to be able to gauge any frustrations or difficulties in their patients' lives. As already mentioned, this can be achieved only by forming a strong relationship with patients and often requires good communication and listening skills, as well as the ability to empathize with the patients' circumstances.

HIV and the MDT

With the deterioration of the immune system, HIV begins attacking various organs of the body, including the gut, liver, lungs, eyes and brain. This indicates progression to AIDS. Numerous doctors from different specialties often see these patients, including GPs, HIV specialists, gastroenterologists, respiratory physicians, ophthalmologists and neurologists among others. They will also be seen by other health professionals, including specialist nurses, speech and language therapists, and social workers. These all work together as a team, combining the concerns that they have elicited to come up with a final care plan. This requires good communication skills to ensure that the various members of the team are working collectively towards achieving the same ultimate goals – to improve the patient's condition and to reduce the impact of HIV/AIDS on daily life.

Prevention of HIV infection

The spread of HIV is not just a medical problem but also a social one, and in this respect requires strong public health action. This involves better education of the public and better use of resources worldwide, as well as breaking down the social stigma attached to the disease.

Treating HIV is a difficult and expensive matter. Although treatment has been successful in prolonging life in the western world and global spending has been increased sixfold, HIV is still out of control in developing countries. Treatment regimens are difficult to adhere to and have a large impact on patients' lives. It is important to look at preventive measures to control this epidemic and to reduce the number of people needing treatment in the future.

The medical community must work with governments to implement global and national programmes to prevent the transmission of HIV by the following:

• Empowering women in societies by education: women are at much greater risk of contracting HIV. Improving access to education will promote their social standing through which they will be able to control sexual practices (for example, demanding condoms, refusing sex and not turning to prostitution), which can reduce transmission rates.

- Educating people about HIV/AIDS through the media and via important figures within communities such as doctors and teachers.
- Promotion of safe sexual practice, especially the importance of barrier methods of contraception.
- Health promotion targeted at high-risk groups such as men who have sex with men and commercial sex workers.
- Establishing good access to HIV testing and treatment.
- Breaking down the stigma attached to HIV.

Stigma in this case is the negative 'labelling' imposed on people with HIV/AIDS as sexually promiscuous and highly infectious individuals, such that they are seen as social outcasts. To a large extent, these beliefs are borne out of ignorance and health-care professionals have a duty to break them down. Such stigma is felt at a personal level and has a major impact on health. For example, someone who has had unprotected sex and wishes to have an HIV test may not do so for fear of being cast out by society because of a positive diagnosis. If this is the case, this individual may have missed an opportunity for early diagnosis and management.

Cancer

We are continually losing cells and replacing them with new ones that carry out the same function. This process of new cell growth (mitosis) is tightly regulated by various cellular mechanisms to ensure that we have the right number of cells and that the new cells carry out their intended function. Cancer is the breakdown of this regulation process where the new cells are dissenters, rendering them harmful tissues to our body. Alarmingly, these cells have the capability to spread, either by damaging normal cells in their vicinity (invasion) or by entering our blood and lymphatic systems to cause damage in a more distant location in the body (metastasis).

This process of normal cells turning 'cancerous' can occur in all parts of the body. To date, over 200 types of cancers have been recognized worldwide. Each of these cancers behaves distinctly and requires different therapeutic measures. It is for this reason that the field of oncology is so diverse and is the focus of large research investment.

The most common cancers in the UK are of the lung, breast, bowel and prostate. This group of cancers account for over half of new cancers occurring in the UK annually, as well as half of all UK cancer deaths.

Treatment of cancer

The diversity of cancers means that there are several different treatment regimens and no single 'magic bullet'. There is no definitive cure for cancer, although a variety of options is currently used depending on the situation:

1. Chemotherapy: this involves the use of drugs with powerful chemical properties that kill cells. Ideally these drugs would be designed with the intention of killing only the cancerous cells, but this is not always the case and can result in damage to healthy tissues.
2. Radiotherapy: this involves the use of ionizing radiation capable of killing cells. This radiation is often delivered via the use of laser guidance and targeted to cancerous tissue.
3. Surgery: the use of surgical techniques to remove cancerous portion from the body to prevent further spread and/or invasion.

The three methods mentioned above are often used simultaneously and it is not uncommon for patients to have chemo- or radiotherapy before and after surgery.

Preventive measures against cancers

Cancer is a complex disease and is often difficult to treat. Although novel therapies have been discovered, cancer continues to account for 1 in 4 deaths in the UK, with annual figures of 150 000. It is of little surprise that so much attention has been put into encouraging the prevention of cancers in the first place. Years of research into the causes of the different cancers have highlighted the importance of making lifestyle modifications that can reduce the incidence of cancers. Although some lifestyle changes are more applicable to certain types of cancers, there are some universal risk factors.

Smoking

This is arguably the most significant risk factor for cancer and simply encouraging patients to quit smoking has been shown to have a significant preventive impact in various cancers. Smoking has a strong correlation to lung cancer and research has shown that cigarettes cause 90% of cases in men and 83% in women. However, several other cancers are also seen more commonly in smokers, such as oesophageal, pharyngeal, oral and liver cancer. Overall, smoking has been shown to cause more than a quarter of all deaths from cancer in the UK.

Diet

Maintaining a diet high in fibre, fruit and vegetables has been shown to have a favourable impact on health and cancer. Reductions in alcohol and red meat consumption have also been shown to be of benefit, as is reducing intake of salt and saturated fats. Should these parameters be achieved it would lead to the maintenance of a healthy body weight, which itself has been shown to be protective against cancer.

Screening programmes

Many common cancers in the UK now have a screening programme installed as part of public health policy. A screening programme is made up of quick and relatively cheap tests that aim to identify individuals who may be at risk of developing cancers. If positive, patients can be investigated early for the relevant cancer and, if required, be treated before the cancer develops or spreads. In this way, it is hoped that the onset of cancer can be prevented. The following are the screening tests currently used in the UK.

Breast cancer

Women aged between 50 and 70 in the UK are screened with a mammogram, an X-ray image of their breast tissue. The aim is to identify individuals who have signs of early breast cancer, and to treat them as soon as possible. The earlier these patients are treated, the higher the chance of cure.

Cervical cancer

Women between 25 and 64 receive a cervical smear test every 3–5 years. This involves taking a sample of cells from the cervix and viewing them under a microscope. The aim is to identify women showing pre-cancerous cells and to treat them accordingly to prevent the development of cancer.

Bowel cancer

Men and women aged between 60 and 69 years old are sent a stool testing kit by post. Samples of faeces are taken by the patient and sent back to be investigated in laboratories for traces of blood, which can indicate bowel tumours. Again the aim is to diagnose and treat potential cancer cases early when cure rates are at their highest.

Screening tests for prostate and ovarian cancers are also being considered, with the latter currently undergoing clinical trials.

In 2008, a cervical cancer vaccine was introduced throughout the UK as a novel preventive measure. Young girls are now immunized against human papillomavirus (HPV), which is associated with 70% of cases. It is hoped that, with time, the number of cases occurring in the UK will be reduced, and that vaccines can be developed against other cancers in the future.

Global aspects

Encouragingly, the number of deaths resulting from cancer in the UK is falling due to the preventive measures implemented and the improvements in treatment methods. This is also true of many other developed countries.

However, cancer is a global concern. Alarmingly, studies have shown that the progress made in the developed world is not reflected in developing countries. It is expected that, in these countries, the number of deaths from cancer is likely to rise, placing an even greater health burden on these societies. Over 80% of children with cancer are believed to live in developing countries. With poor urban populations in countries such as India and China adopting lifestyles with higher smoking rates, less exercise and poorer diets, there is an urgent need to rectify these issues.

There appears to be little interest in introducing preventive measures and, when it comes to treatment, due to the high prices imposed by pharmaceutical companies, highly effective drugs are unavailable for the population.

Advances in molecular biology

Developments in the field of genetics in the last century have opened many new avenues for research and introduced new directions in the treatment of medical conditions. Traditional methods of therapy revolved around drugs that mimic and manipulate physiological functions in the body, or surgical intervention. After the completion of the Human Genome Project, we now know the chromosome location and nucleotide sequence of many genes. Currently, research is being undertaken to identify the function of these genes and their involvement in diseases. The hope and long-term aim are that a disease can be cured by targeting the root of the error and 'correcting' these genes.

Medical genetics, as this field has now come to be known, presents many ethical and moral debates. This is particularly the case in the field of stem cell research and human cloning.

Human cloning and stem cell research

The famous sheep, 'Dolly', was successfully cloned in 1997. This was a breakthrough in the field of molecular biology and raised interest in the possibility of cloning humans and, more immediately, cloning human tissues from embryonic stem cells. It is hoped that, in the future, embryonic cells can be isolated and subsequently manipulated to form specific tissues for damaged organs. Potential areas where stem cells may be particularly valuable are in tissue replacement in burns, heart disease and degenerative neurological diseases.

There are many arguments against the field of cloning and its integration into medicine:

- Cloning is a relatively new field and the biological functions of stem cell-derived tissues remain questionable. This is exemplified by the fact that Dolly the sheep herself suffered from premature arthritis and died at just 6 years of age due to lung disease. It must be noted, however, that it has never been proven that the lung disease was a consequence of cloning. Nevertheless, whether we can afford to take such risks in human hosts needs to be carefully considered.
- Biotechnology companies seeking public investment are exploiting the hype surrounding cloning.
- When obtaining stem cells, embryos, which are potential lives, are exterminated. Is this termination of life? There are powerful lobby groups that believe that humans should not have the power to experiment with embryonic stem cells.
- There is a fear that the use of cloning will progress beyond medical use and lead to commercial cloning of human beings, for example, creating 'cosmetic babies' with preselected features.
- There may be legal issues surrounding the ownership and identity of embryonic-derived tissue.

Ischaemic heart disease

Ischaemic heart disease (IHD) is a cardiovascular disease. An organ is deemed 'ischaemic' when its blood supply is insufficient. An example of this is coronary artery disease (CAD), where the narrowing of the lumen of the coronary arteries causes inadequate perfusion to the heart muscle.

Ischaemic heart disease (IHD) is the most common cause of death in the UK, and recent data show that approximately one in five men and one in six women will die from the condition. Furthermore, roughly 101 000 people die each year from IHD in the UK, which is among the highest death rates in Europe. In financial terms, coronary artery disease (CAD) costs the NHS £7.9 billion each year, which is equivalent to 8% of its annual budget. Judging by those statistics, it is clear that IHD is a massive burden on the health of the UK population, with an equally significant burden on the NHS's finite resources. On a more positive note, over the last 10 years, the death rate from CAD in those under the age of 65 has fallen by 46% due to improvements in treatment and prevention.

Atherosclerosis

Arterial occlusions are the result of the formation of atheroma – plaques that are filled with cholesterol and inflammatory cells in the inner lining of the artery. The process of atheroma formation is known as 'atherosclerosis'.

Atherosclerosis is a gradual process that takes place over decades and does not manifest itself symptomatically until very late in its development.

It begins when normal cells lining blood vessels (endothelium) become damaged, either mechanically as a result of high blood pressure or chemically by toxins such as smoking. An inflammatory reaction occurs which is mediated by the immune system and certain white blood cells are attracted to the site of damage. These cells absorb low-density lipoproteins (LDLs) or 'bad cholesterol' in the bloodstream, forming a plaque within the blood vessels. As this grows, a thick fibrous tissue forms on the plaque, called the 'fibrous cap'.

The fibrous cap is unstable and, with time, it wears down and can rupture or crack. This exposes the plaque to inflammatory cells in the blood and immediately leads to the formation of a blood clot within the artery (thrombosis) at the site of rupture. The clot can potentially block the blood flow in the artery, and therefore the supply of oxygen to any organ dependent on that artery becomes inadequate, leading to ischaemia. If the coronary arteries are affected, the result is a myocardial infarction (heart attack), whereas if the artery supplying the brain is affected, the individual suffers a stroke.

Risk factors

Modifiable risk factors for IHD relate to a person's lifestyle, while non-modifiable factors are fixed (Table 11.2).

Unhealthy lifestyles

The concern is that a lot of the modifiable risk factors are becoming increasingly prevalent around the world at younger ages than in previous generations. This is certainly the case with increasing numbers of obese children, and the unhealthy fast food culture that leads to an increase in cholesterol levels. This accelerates the atherosclerotic process and put individuals at a greater risk of myocardial infarctions and strokes.

Furthermore, the increased consumption of fast foods is coupled with a decrease in physical activity. It is recommended that a person should do a minimum of 30 minutes of exercise at least five times a week, but this has been made difficult by occupational

Table 11.2 Risk factors for ischaemic heart disease (IHD)

Modifiable risk factors	Non-modifiable risk factors
Smoking	Family history
Obesity	Male sex
Lack of physical activity	Old age
Unhealthy diet: high in saturated fats/salt	Early menopause
Excess alcohol	Ethnicity (highest risk in people from south-east Asia)

Treatable risk factors	
High blood pressure	
High cholesterol	
Diabetes	

habits. Data from the British Heart Foundation show that, in the UK, a third of adults exercise only once a week at most. Healthy foods are also proportionately more expensive than unhealthy foods, making them more inaccessible to poorer groups.

Smoking

It is said that smoking one pack a day over a significant period can more than double the risk of a myocardial infarction. Overall, 14% of cardiovascular-related deaths in men and 12% in women are attributable to smoking. More people die prematurely from cardiovascular conditions as a result of smoking before they will have even developed lung cancer.

Smoking has a great influence on atherosclerosis. First, toxic chemicals damage the endothelium, as discussed earlier, and this acts as the initiator for atheroma formation. Second, smoking increases the concentration of LDL-cholesterol in the blood, which again is one of the key ingredients in formation of atherosclerotic plaques. Finally, it increases the likelihood of clots forming in the blood.

Any effort to prevent IHD must include smoking cessation policies, because smoking is the single most important modifiable risk factor. Recently the government has taken steps by banning smoking in public places, while smoking cessation clinics are becoming increasingly available in primary care.

High blood pressure

High blood pressure, also known as hypertension, is a significant risk factor because it is one of the initiators of endothelial damage in the first stage of atherosclerosis. Hypertension also puts an increased strain on the heart, which leads to an increased oxygen demand and may eventually lead to heart failure.

It can be controlled by a variety of drugs as well as through weight loss and regular physical activity. GPs are strongly encouraged to be active in lowering the blood pressure of their patients, and there are specific guidelines on the appropriate use of drugs.

High cholesterol

Another controllable risk factor is a high cholesterol level in the blood. LDL-cholesterol is an important component of atheromatous plaques, and therefore high levels in the blood accelerate their formation and growth. This risk factor is heavily influenced by diets that are high in saturated fats such as cheese, butter, full-cream milk and fried food.

A class of drugs called statins are currently widely used to reduce the LDL concentration in the blood and improve lipid profiles. They have been shown to decrease mortality from cardiovascular disease. They are prescribed to people who have risk factors of heart disease, even if their cholesterol levels are 'normal'. Some sections of the medical professions think wider use of the drug in the population should be considered.

Type 2 diabetes

Type 2 diabetes typically occurs in adulthood as a result of defective insulin secretion by the pancreas and resistance by target tissues. Insulin is required to control blood glucose, which at high levels can be toxic. The condition is strongly correlated with obesity and the diabetes epidemic is predicted to affect 336 million people around the world by 2030 if current trends continue, with most countries ill-equipped to deal with this problem.

As a result of the unhealthy lifestyles and obesity in younger individuals, it is becoming increasingly prevalent among children. In some parts of the world, type 2 diabetes is a greater concern in children than type 1 diabetes (a condition that presents in childhood).

Diabetes can lead to complications such as CAD, kidney failure, blindness and amputation. Treatment can be with insulin replacement, as well as a variety of other drugs, and the aim is to control blood glucose. However, the cost of treatment and the impact of morbidity on an individual's life can make diabetes a serious economic burden on societies. It is further reason for better preventive measures against obesity.

Treatment of IHD

The management and prevention of IHD can initially be divided into two categories: primary and secondary.

Primary management is essentially changes by the affected individual with regard to lifestyle, including smoking cessation, regular physical activity and eating a healthy diet. It is important to stress that changes in lifestyle can have a bigger effect than any form of medication. Therefore any attempt by a clinician to treat a patient with IHD is futile unless accompanied by considerable changes to their way of life as detailed earlier.

Secondary management involves the clinician managing the patient's risk factors and IHD with the use of a variety of medications that are of substantial benefit, provided that they are used early enough. If a person has symptoms of angina or is considered to be at high risk for whatever reason, they can be prescribed a combination of drugs, including:

- statins: to reduce cholesterol levels in the blood
- antihypertensives: aim to reduce blood pressure
- anticoagulants: thin the blood and prevent clot formation; these are widely prescribed to people at risk of IHD

Patients tend to have a cluster of risk factors, and therefore the above medications are often given together to good effect, especially in conjunction with primary prevention.

The 'Polypill'

The 'Polypill', which has been well covered in the media, is a combination of the above drugs given as one tablet. The Polypill could prove to be a significant advancement in the management of IHD and its risk factors for several reasons. First, it combines five drugs into one pill, which will make it much more convenient for patients and will increase adherence to medication. Second, if given at a younger age to people who do not have symptoms, their risk of developing cardiovascular disease may be reduced in the long term. Finally, the five drugs that make the Polypill are cheap and therefore this represents a potentially cost-effective measure of preventing heart disease. It is currently undergoing clinical trials, although, as the component ingredients are off patent, pharmaceutical companies are showing little interest in the drug, because it does not have as great a profit margin as individual drugs.

Public health initiatives

Given that heart disease affects so many people around the world, it represents a very significant public health challenge. Given the close link between how we live our lives and our risk of developing cardiovascular disease, tackling this massive problem begins with education at a young age, encouraging children to eat healthily and exercise. However, for this to materialize, incentives need to be provided such as better access to recreational facilities and subsidies on healthier foods. The wider public also need to be more informed with regard to their risk profile, and know how this can be reduced.

Swine influenza

The swine influenza (A/H1N1) outbreak began in Mexico in March 2009. Originally a respiratory disease found in pigs, the virus has since evolved and spread to humans. In June 2009, the World Health Organization (WHO) declared that the disease had reached pandemic proportions. At present, most cases that have been recorded are in the USA and in Mexico, followed by Australia, Chile and the UK. In the UK, spread of the disease has been mainly concentrated around institutions such as schools and, so far, the effects have been moderate. However, a primary concern of WHO is the impact of swine influenza in less developed countries. Due to inadequate healthcare systems and the prevalence of major diseases such as malnutrition, diabetes and HIV/AIDS, an outbreak of the disease could be devastating and difficult to control.

The symptoms of swine influenza are similar to those experienced during seasonal influenza, although it has demonstrated faster rates of infection amongst people under the age of 50. Those who are thought to be infected are advised to stay at home and avoid social contact, including visits to GP surgeries or hospitals, until recovery. In July 2009, the NHS launched the National Pandemic Flu Service, with the aim of further taking the pressure off GP surgeries by encouraging people who suspect they have swine influenza to answer a short questionnaire online or over the telephone about their symptoms and medical history. If their answers suggest that they do have swine influenza, they may be advised to take the antiviral drug oseltamivir (Tamiflu), and someone will be authorized to collect it on their behalf. This measure was taken partly in response to the unregulated sale of the drug online, as Tamiflu is only recommended for use in severely ill patients and those who have underlying medical conditions. There are, however, some concerns that this service will result in excessive use of Tamiflu, leading to antiviral resistance and the depletion of supplies.

Some epidemiologists worry that the current strain of the virus, by continuing to spread, will evolve into a more elusive and dangerous form with fears of many more deaths. This fear stems from the pattern of the 1918 influenza pandemic, which killed at least 50 million people of which 96% were in low- or middle-income areas. It is hoped that a more effective vaccine against swine influenza will be produced in time to curb such an event.

Controlling the spread of swine influenza requires public health vigilance and action at all levels including WHO, national governments, local governments and public institutions, with the utmost importance in developing decisive and effective policies as well as communicating accurate information that the public can adhere to, as and when the threat arises. This may involve encouraging those who are infected, or who have come in contact with virus, to maintain isolation for a period of time, wearing face masks and closing down public spaces such as schools, universities and hospitals.

12 Off the beaten track

With Veena Naganathar and Susannah Love

A number of initiatives have recently been introduced to make medicine a more accessible career for a broader spectrum of people. As well as increasing opportunities, these steps in the right direction have allowed people with a variety of skills and life experiences into the fold.

Widening participation

The medical profession has been strongly encouraged to take on doctors who reflect the communities that they serve. However, due to grassroots inequalities in education, it remains most accessible for students from higher socioeconomic groups. To challenge this state of play, some medical schools have tried to redress this balance, although there is a long way to go if targets to reflect diversity are to be met.

Medicine should not be ruled out as a career option if you are outperforming your peers in your school or college, even if it is unrealistic for you to achieve the standard entry requirements expected by most medical schools. For instance, if you are studying biology and chemistry (at least one to A2 level) and you have been predicted BBC (with another B at AS level), and this is 60% higher than the average performance at your school or college, you will be eligible for interview at St George's University of London for the standard 5-year course.

Extended medical courses

Other medical schools offer an extended medical course for students who are unable to meet entry requirements but meet certain socioeconomic criteria. All of these schools expect satisfactory completion of UKCAT (Table 12.1).

Table 12.1 Requirements for extended medical courses

Medical school	Minimum requirements	Subjects
East Anglia	A levels: BCC IB: 29 points BTEC Level 3 National Diploma in Health and Social Care: DDM www.uea.ac.uk/med/course/6mbms	Any subjects Health studies
King's	Three A levels: BCC + one AS level or Two A levels: BC + CCE in three AS levels www.kcl.ac.uk/ugp10/programme/687	Chemistry to A2 level Biology/Mathematics/Physics to at least AS level
Nottingham[a]	A levels: CCC Access course/BTEC level 3 www.lincoln.ac.uk/fabs/_courses/undergraduate/health_science/default.asp	Biology + chemistry Biology + chemistry content
Southampton	A levels: CCC or A levels: CC + BB in AS-level biology and chemistry www.som.soton.ac.uk/undergraduates/bm6/	Biology + chemistry

[a]A preliminary year is spent obtaining a Certificate in Health Science at the University at Lincoln before transferring to Year 1 Medicine at the University of Nottingham.

Evidence from King's College London has demonstrated the success of extended medical programmes in the UK, and the degree that is obtained is of the same value as that obtained in the standard course. For further information, see: www.bmj.com/cgi/content/full/336/7653/1111?view=long&pmid=18483054.

In addition, there are smaller local initiatives offered by some of the other medical schools. You could speak to your careers adviser or the admission tutor at your local medical school to see if there is anything that may be accessible for you.

Access courses

Access courses are designed to improve the applications of students who wish to go into medicine or other similar courses, but lack the conventional entry requirements. They are usually aimed at people over the age of 19. Table 12.2 is a list of access courses, as well as the medical schools that will consider students who complete them successfully.

Barts and The London, Bristol, Cambridge and Glasgow medical schools are also willing to consider students who have successfully completed an access course. To clarify the conditions of admission, you should contact the admissions office at your preferred medical schools.

Graduate entry medicine

What do a 32-year-old jeweller, a 26-year-old social worker, a 38-year-old fitness instructor and a 28-year-old tax consultant all have in common? On a sunny July afternoon, they all graduated from medical school, after completing a graduate entry medical course.

Graduate entry medical courses are a relatively new concept in the UK after being introduced by St George's University of London and Warwick Medical School in 2000. Since then, they have expanded to being offered by 16 UK medical schools. Teaching medicine exclusively to graduates is not a new idea; in the USA, all medical degrees are graduate entry only, and Australia has been running graduate entry courses for over a decade.

Graduate entry courses were designed to overcome the shortfall in numbers of doctors by encouraging applications to courses from a previously untapped but rich resource. Graduate students are an attractive prospect for medical schools; their days of teenage angst are long gone (although mid-life crises might be just around the corner) and they are a highly motivated and committed group of students with invaluable real-life skills and experiences.

Table 12.2 Requirements for Access courses

Access course	Medical schools
University of Bradford Clinical Sciences www.brad.ac.uk/acad/clinsci	Leeds
City and Islington College Medicine and Allied Profession Access to Higher Education Level 3 www.candi.ac.uk/courses/factsheet.aspx? coursechoice=AS2232A09&strgroup=ad	
City College Norwich Access to Medicine www.ccn.ac.uk/ccn3/general/coursedetails. asp?id=3392	Brighton and Sussex, Cardiff, East Anglia, Hull–York, Keele, King's, Leeds, Leicester, Liverpool, Newcastle, Sheffield, Southampton
Lambeth College OCNLR Access to Higher Education Diploma: Medicine, Dentistry, Radiography and Medical Biosciences – Medicine and Biomedical Science www.lambethcollege.ac.uk/adults/course_list.cfm? widCall1=customWidgets.courses_list_courseDetail& cit_id=492&cta_tax_id=626&showCourseKey=true	St Andrew's
University of Leeds Interdisciplinary Science Foundation Programme (CFG0) www.leeds.ac.uk/cjh/foundation/index.htm	Leeds
University of Liverpool Foundation to Health Studies www.liv.ac.uk/healthsciences/undergrad/guidance_notes.htm	Liverpool
Manchester College of Arts and Technology Access to HE Diploma: Medicine www.mancat.ac.uk/adult/courses/course_details.asp?sa= a01&cat=oracle&index=CR3341-01&leaflet=103&cat=oracle	Aberdeen
Perth College HNC Applied Sciences (Pathway to Medicine) www.perth.uhi.ac.uk/courses/Pages/U00FC_F1_PB.aspx	St Andrew's
Sussex Downs College www.sussexdowns.ac.uk/Page/Show/AccesstoMedicine	Brighton and Sussex, UEA, Hull–York, Leeds, Liverpool, Newcastle, St George's
Thames Valley University Pre-medical option (Certificate of Higher Education) http://courses.tvu.ac.uk – type 'pre-medical option' into search	Imperial
College of West Anglia Access to Medicine and Dentistry www.col-westanglia.ac.uk/pdfs/Access_to_ Medicine_and_Dentistry-8960.pdf	Aberdeen, Brighton and Sussex, East Anglia, Edinburgh, Hull–York, Keele, King's, Leicester, Leeds, Liverpool, Manchester, Newcastle, Oxford, Sheffield, Southampton, St Andrew's, St George's, UCL

NB Barts and The London, Bristol, Cambridge, and Glasgow are willing to consider all access courses.

What is the difference between a mature student and a graduate student?

Mature students are those over 21 years of age who have not previously graduated from a university. Mature students who wish to study medicine are eligible to apply to undergraduate medical courses in the usual way, as they have done for many years.

Graduate students are those who already hold a university degree. They are eligible to apply for the 4-year, 'fast-track', graduate entry medical courses. They are also eligible to apply to most undergraduate medical courses, but a few medical schools that run both undergraduate and graduate courses allow graduate students to apply only to their graduate programmes.

The graduate entry medical course

Graduate entry medical courses are 4-year 'fast-track' programmes designed exclusively for graduate students. Most graduate courses are run in parallel with the undergraduate course at the same university. The graduate students are taught on a separate fast-track pre-clinical phase (usually 12–18 months) to their undergraduate colleagues, and the courses are then integrated from the start of clinical studies. The exceptions to this rule are Swansea and Warwick medical schools, which exclusively run 4-year courses. Candidates should bear in mind, however, that the graduate courses are more competitive than the standard courses because there are fewer places available. At some medical schools, those who are unsuccessful at graduate entry will be automatically considered for the 5-year course, but this is not always the case.

Graduate courses have many advantages over traditional undergraduate courses. They are shorter in length: 4 years compared with 5- or 6-year courses. The pre-clinical phase is usually shortened to accommodate the reduction in course length. Course content is not compromised and so the pre-clinical phase is more intensive compared with standard undergraduate courses. The courses are designed for a more mature mind, with a great deal of self-directed learning, which can suit most graduate students. Another major advantage is that, from Year 2 onwards, students on graduate entry courses receive an NHS bursary, including payment of fees and travel reimbursement.

All graduate entry programmes have to cover the same core content as the undergraduate courses to meet GMC requirements and the final qualification is equivalent to that of a longer medical course. Any concerns about being viewed as a 'second-class' doctor for studying medicine on a graduate entry course are completely unfounded.

Entry requirements and exams

All the medical schools that offer a graduate programme require the applicant to possess a degree, but there is some variation regarding acceptability of degree class and discipline (Table 12.3). Most universities have a similar selection process for the graduate courses as the undergraduate courses, namely the

Table 12.3 Entry requirements for graduate entry

Medical school	Degree requirement	Entrance test
Barts and The London	2:1 in science degree	UKCAT
Birmingham	2:1 in life science degree	
Bristol	2:1 in biomedical science degree	
Cambridge	2:1 in any discipline	
Imperial	2:1 or PhD in biological subject	UKCAT
Keele	2:1 in any discipline	GAMSAT
King's	2:1 in any discipline	UKCAT
Leicester	2:1 in any discipline	UKCAT
Liverpool	2:1 in biomedical/health science degree	
Newcastle	2:1 in any discipline	UKCAT
Nottingham	2:2 in any discipline	GAMSAT
Oxford	2:1 in applied or experimental science degree	UKCAT
Southampton	2:1 in any discipline	UKCAT
St George's	2:2 in any discipline	GAMSAT
Swansea	2:1 in any discipline	GAMSAT
Warwick	2:1 in science degree	UKCAT

By which they mean a first.

UCAS application form and the UKCAT exam followed by an interview. A few universities, however, require the applicant to sit the GAMSAT (Graduate Australian Medical School Admissions Test) (see Chapter 8) before being shortlisted for interview.

When faced with all the complexities and excitement of planning your application to medical school, don't forget about planning how you are going to fund your studies, especially if you are used to earning a comfortable salary. The expenses faced by any student include living expenses, tuition fees, course books and travel expenses. Graduate students may have other expenses to consider, such as mortgages, debts from their first degree, or other financial responsibilities such as partners and children. Holidays are significantly shorter on all medical courses and so it will not be possible to rely on holiday jobs to top up your bank account.

Non-science students

If you have completed non-science A levels or are a non-science graduate, you could consider applying for a premedical course. This will be a 6-year course with a 'Year 0' that normally covers basic biomedical sciences, while students progress to Year 1 of the conventional course on completion. Universities that offer these courses are Bristol, Cardiff, Dundee, Keele, Kingston (who transfer to St George's for Year 1), Manchester and Sheffield.

Re-sits

If you didn't get the grades the first time around, you should contact the admissions officers at the medical schools to which you applied and see what other options may be open to you. If you have extenuating circumstances, you may be able to re-apply with grades from A-level re-sits, but generally this is not accepted. You should consider applying to an access course or another university degree through which you may be able to enter medicine as a graduate.

Index